return to RADIANCE

THE RESTORATIVE SUPERPOWERS OF DIAMOND GRACE

TERRI GERVAIS

Edited by Laurie Knight

Cover Design by Jessica Murrell

SCRIBES OF LIGHT
P R E S S

An Imprint for GracePoint Publishing (www.GracePointPublishing.com)

GracePoint Matrix, LLC
624 S. Cascade Ave
Suite 201
Colorado Springs, CO 80903
www.GracePointMatrix.com
Email: Admin@GracePointMatrix.com
SAN # 991-6032

A Library of Congress Control Number has been requested and is pending.

ISBN: (Paperback) 978-1-955272-25-4

eISBN: 978-1-955272-90-2

Books may be purchased for educational, business, or sales promotional use.

For bulk order requests and price schedule contact:

Orders@GracePointPublishing.com

Praise for *Return to Radiance*

Return to Radiance: The Restorative Superpowers of Diamond Grace is an exquisite symphony of divine light, love, and grace. As our planet continues to evolve to a greater paradigm expression, we are also invited to claim a new state of who eness. *Return to Radiance* delivers a high frequency upleveling experience that is a match for our divine expression to be lived now. If you feel the stirrings of your soul that call you to live and BE the contribution you came here for, this work is a treasure trove that makes a difference. Terri speaks from the leading edge of the sacred, as a stand for transformation, elevated consciousness that serves all creation and living a life informed by the light of our divine nature, where wellness and wholeness are fully expressed at every level of being.

Darlene Green
Author of *In Service to Love: A Dynamic Experience of Consciousness, Transformation, and Enlightenment*

I've loved the immersive experience of reading *Return to Radiance*. I re-read a chapter and then a new insight catches my eye. I find myself evolving and growing further along the pathway to renewed well-being and grace. Usually I read intently, and only once. With this book new insights unravel with every return. That's because I find the energy which pours forth is deliciously tangible and empowering. I put the book down feeling better in my Self than when I started!

Sejual Shah
Executive Coach and EFT Trainer
www.healthyinmind.com

I enjoy it immensely, really. It is very very powerful for me, almost sentence by sentence deeply infused and deeply resonant in activating and initiating and very touching. As if I have "waited" for this for a long time. A lot makes deeper sense now, I mean a deeper understanding of my life. And excitement for what is to come. To bring this grace geometry and energy alive on earth. I really thank you deeeeeply. I send you my love and gratefulness.

Judith H.

Contents

Foreword From Thoth

(as Divinely Transmitted by Danielle Rama Hoffman)

Hello Dear Ones,

This is Thoth and Infinite Oneness moving more to the forefront of this Divine Transmission. We are delighted you have found your way to these pages. As you're settling in, we invite you to take a moment to acknowledge that you have found this book for a reason and that reason, like a diamond, is multi-faceted. First and foremost, you are here to reclaim radiance and grace for yourself, and to enjoy the ripple effect of a return to radiance in your life.

Radiance restores grace to your physical body by reversing aging and physical dis-ease and by reclaiming youthfulness, vitality, wellness, and beauty. Radiance brings coherence to your emotions, thoughts, and words, which overflows into being a creator of your most exquisite life. Your journey in these pages takes you directly into an inner state of graceful radiance that directly impacts your health, beauty, joy, abundance, relation-ships, mission, contribution to others, and all the facets of your gem of a life.

Your primary reason for being here is to create incredible changes for you personally, yet your radiance does not stop there. This brings us to the second reason you are here, which is much bigger. It is to be a part of the larger contribution in raising consciousness on Earth and her inhabitants, and to support the Earth (and to receive the support of Earth) as she also journeys to resurrect grace and radiance to restore the animals, water, air, soil, trees, and your fellow Earth walkers to radiant wellness.

You're here to connect to a galactic level of radiance and support that is what your author Terri describes as *Diamond Grace*, where you, the Earth, and the cosmos are aligned with radiance. The mere fact that you're here and you're reading this is an indication that you have a Divine appointment to be on this team as an ambassador of the radiance of Diamond Grace, and to be a location of Diamond Grace. The words, the pages of this book, the rejuvenation meditations, the affirmations, the awakening of different aspects of grace, and the facets of you as a diamond are all aligning you to this return of grace.

It is not only Terri who has this mission to return grace to the Earth Star, but it is also you, too. You also have this mission to return grace and radiance, zest for life, vivaciousness, energy, and radiance. So, to know that as you find yourself on these pages, you are called to be here for a reason. You have a role in the return of grace to the Earth. We are delighted that you are here, and you are not alone.

You are supported by not only the wider Diamond Grace group of ambassadors on Earth, but also many Light Beings, guides, and Ascended Masters.

This book is light-infused, with the sacred geometry of Diamond Grace energetically imbued within it. Your journey in this book is a session. It is a resurrection of Diamond Grace which was dormant for a very long time. It is an initiation. We as a Council of Light Beings have a primary partnership and agreement to bring this forward. Know that this is a team effort.

We are delighted that you are here, and you will not be the same when you complete this resurrection journey as when you begin it, you will be even more of you in your most concentrated self. The years of pressure, time, and separation consciousness (just like carbon becomes a diamond) have refined you. The resurrection of Diamond Grace is like the unearthing, then the polishing of that diamond. You have been a diamond forming in the rough, and now it's time for you to be that diamond in grace. We are excited to bring you this journey; we are honored and blessed to be a Divine partner with you, with Diamond Grace, with the Earth Star, and with the evolution in consciousness.

chapter one

Let the Journey Begin

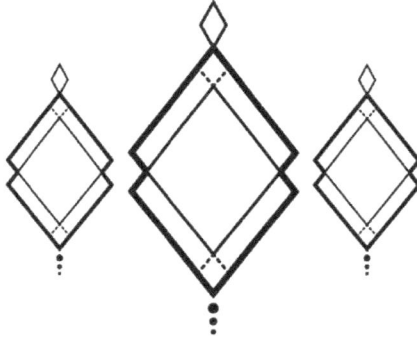

Open to Receive the Energetic Transmission Within

You are invited to enter into Diamond Grace like entering through a temple door, a sacred space. It is also like entering into a session that you might have with a practitioner where you are entering with an open heart, knowing that you are always guiding the process. You're choosing what to take from this journey. As you are reading, taking the words in through your eyes and your optic nerve and your pineal gland located within your physical brain, you're holding the book in your hands—you may even place it on your heart at some point—know that there is this energy package that is bespoke to you to support you in your resurrection of grace. Like osmosis, where the cells cross information from one another, this is a transmission of energy. It is a transmission of knowledge from many Ascended Masters who have walked this path and are supporting this work.

This book has descended from the higher dimensional planes above the Earth Star where it is written in Light Language and Love Language. It is written in frequencies, vibrations, and sound. As it was being birthed into the third dimension through the hands, voice, eyes, along with the frequencies and vibrations emanating from the scribe, everything was preserved and divinely infused energetically and physically into the pages of this book. If there are concepts, ideas, information that you have never heard before, or that you have been taught to be false, we invite you to consider that perhaps those before you weren't ready for this information. When you open the book, you are walking between the dimensions, and in doing so you will change. You are immersing yourself in this Source Light and Love Language.

You're not only reading these channeled words with your eyes, but also your hands are reading them similarly to braille. You probably have not heard that this is possible, but it is. It is an infusion of truth, of Divine truth, of words of wisdom, power, and love. These light-encoded words and sacred geometry shapes are sparking an internal knowing of your Source of origin. It is sparking and illuminating the dormant biological processes within your physical body. As you light up and absorb these frequencies, vibrations, and sacred geometries, you are resurrecting these sacred geometries within your own energetic body. These shapes have been called, or are known as Tetrahedrons, Merkaba, Metatron's Cube, the Flower of Life, and/or the Seed of Life.

These are the fundamental blueprints for all of creation in the cosmic universe, and you are connecting to this state of perfection. You are aligning your physical body to Source. As you illuminate these sacred geometries, you are illuminating yourself to be a Diamond Grace portal of which you are now a connector point to the Earth's grid, the grid of Diamond Grace around the Earth. This is important work. You are becoming a shining diamond beacon for grace. You are emanating and resurrecting grace all around your physical environment. You are radiating these frequencies and light codes for all to feel and to infuse a Divine knowing, a familiarity in everyone around you. They may not see it yet, but you are emanating a love that has been absent from the Earth Star for millions of years. As you evolve, you are assisting this evolution in consciousness for the Earth Star, for the Goddess of the Earth, Gaia, and for your Divine Mother/Father in the universe.

This book itself is a portal for Diamond Grace. As you read, feel the radiance of these pages aligning you with your true self. We are so grateful if you choose to participate in the resurrection of Diamond Grace within your own physical body and for the environment around you, as you are restoring the lands that you walk upon to a state of perfection. The pages of this book will assist your journey into wholeness and back into a state of grace. Diamond Grace is a grid overlaying the Earth Star, and it is a representation of the dormancy that lies within your physical body. By reading these words, holding the light-infused matter in your hands, and thereby activating Diamond Grace, you are helping to restore this Earth Star to its perfect creation.

Become a State of Grace in Your Daily Life

Wholeness is all the parts of you illuminating, radiating with light. Wholeness is bringing all the pieces and parts of you that were abandoned, forgotten, cast away, and brought back into this embodiment and forgiven. Forgive yourself; forgive all actions that have occurred in your lifetime, and in any lifetime your essence may have had upon this Earth Star. Bring all the parts back into oneness, back into the center of your heart where they can be loved and forgiven, honored, and resourced to strengthen your physical body. Bring them so you can forgive and love your emotions that are affecting your emotional body, to release judgment upon yourself, your thoughts or your emotions or your actions or deeds. Bring them all in and love every part of yourself.

When you have given yourself this grace, you can emanate it to others as you forgive and cease passing judgment. You honor the life they live and all the lives they've lived. You honor all species on the Earth Star, and all species in the cosmic universe. You become a state of grace. Allow the grace of the Divine Mother to enter your heart and feel what it is like to have a drop of grace. This nurturing, loving state of grace is your birthright. It is you coming into alignment with your true self.

Are You Creating from a State of Grace?

Ways to acknowledge that you are creating from a state of grace will show up in your daily life. For example, you may be driving in traffic, and someone cuts you off, and you do not react. You just relax and let it go. It could be a confrontation with a loved one approaching you and accusing you of hurting them or they get angry, and you do not respond with harsh words. You just sit with a gentle heart and listen with compassion. You hear the words. You pause your voice, and you allow them to offload these deep-seated emotions.

As you allow them to voice this, they are releasing out of their emotional body, and it is healing them. If you act with love and a warm embrace, you are diffusing the situation. You will know when you are coming in resonance with grace. These opportunities will arise, and you will have many opportunities to discover your physical state of grace as you too are off-loading these deep-seated emotions. If you do find yourself in a reactionary state, allow the grace within to acknowledge that you too are clearing out what is unpreferred energy and emotions and you are allowing more units of grace, of light, to radiate within.

The journey to a state of grace is not instantaneous. Your journey away from grace has been for millions of years (although many believe this to be only hundreds of thousands of years, and some even believe it be just thousands of years). If this is new to you, simply allow it to sit and consider. Be gentle with yourself on your journey back. You are clearing these deep-seated wounds not only for yourself but for all humanity on the Earth Star. We acknowledge your presence. We acknowledge the inner work that you are doing, and we are grateful. We are assisting you in many, many ways to bring this process back to grace with ease.

Remember that some concepts presented here bring a new understanding and explanation and your conditioning might push back a bit. If it does, take a break by holding the book against your heart. When the time is right, you will continue reading.

Rejoice in the Process and Restore Your Body

As you resurrect the sacred geometry of grace, you will experience subtle, perhaps imperceptible, changes within your three-dimensional self; your bone structure will come into alignment with this innate perfection and bring the physical body into symmetry, balance, and strength. There could be what might feel like pain or aches as the body is recalibrating to its original Divine blueprint. Your experience of this can be "up-leveled" by your thoughts and your words acknowledging your return to the Divine blueprint, the perfectly balanced body, and rejoicing in gratitude for the process occurring within your system. Your body is listening. Be gentle with yourself.

We need you to know there are elementals within your physical body moving through your bloodstream, lymphatic system, and cells and tissues. These are multifaceted crystals and microscopic life that are helping to restore this state of perfection and they respond to your love and your gratitude. This is the most optimal way of restoration. This is the most optimal way to experience the realignment, for returning to a state of grace is inclusive of your mind, body, and your emotions. All is one. When they are aligned, the light can fuse. Your light body can fuse with your physical body when all is in alignment. This is called *divine fusion*. The energetic patterns merge into alignment. This process cannot be instantaneous as it would be too much on the physical body. This process, done with ease and grace, may take a while in your time on the Earth Star. Allow it to be and acknowledge the process.

Preparing Your System to Resurrect Grace and Radiance

As you begin your journey in this sacred text, you are invited to come into a place of the zero point, to bring coherence to the facets of you: your body, mind, and emotions. The zero point is a term known for absence, absence of imperfection. This is the point where diamonds are created. When your physical body is absent of all that is not serving to support you (dross or negative thoughts or emotions, drama, and trauma and the leftover traces of such) it creates a zero point, and within this state, the carbon in your physical body becomes crystalline, like a diamond.

chapter two

The Diamond Grace Grid

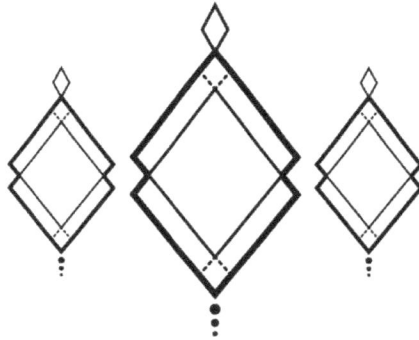

The Resurrection of Your Creative Power Centers

The Diamond Grace grid encompasses the surface of the Earth Star in a sacred geodesic pattern. It is undetectable by the human eye. It is anchored below the surface of the Earth and as a reflection in light above the Earth Star. At certain junctures where these grid lines meet, a vortex is created. It is also a sacred geometry vortex. It is connected by triangles that represent the facets of the diamond. These vortexes are portals or locations that reach through the atmosphere of your Earth and allow beings across the Multiverse to come and go safely into the lower atmosphere of the Earth and into the Earth Star herself.

There is much activity in these areas. They are like a space station on the Earth Star where many Beings of Light and Love can come and support the Starseeds that are on the Earth at this now moment. Many Starseeds are walking upon the surface of the Earth in this time frame, and they are here to assist the evolution of humanity. These portals and access points for other star beings have been present on the Earth Star since the beginning of the Earth herself, but over time many of these portals became dormant. After 2012, it was time to relight or resurrect these portals.

Many other Beings of Light exist on other planets in your solar system as well as beyond, and they are here to assist all. They are here as benevolent beings. They are here to help calm the Earth Star, and to help ease the catastrophic events that are occurring. They are here to help the Earth, and they are here to help all of us. There are many books that have brought messages to you to educate you and get you familiar with who they are. They are inviting you to welcome them into your awareness.

We live in one solar system different from yours. We are in unity and unison with each other. What is occurring on the Earth Star is reverberating out into your solar system. Each planet affects the other and bringing about peace and grace on the Earth is very much desired by all in your solar system. These beings are coming and going through these access points into the lower atmosphere of the Earth Star. There is a grid that mirrors the planetary surface, a circular planetary surface as above so below, above the Earth, and below the Earth. Within these are upward-facing diamonds and downward-facing diamonds, and the access points together meet at the surface of the Earth.

Some of these portals are for space travel and some are for a light infusion of support from the light outside of the Earth Star that has been untouched. It has not been requalified. It is pure nourishing light from your fifth-dimensional sun and from the ascended guides that are here to assist us in raising our frequency and vibrations and raising the light quotient upon the

Earth Star. Your dark days, your dark ages, are over.

Illumination of Your DNA and Regeneration of Earth's Resources

This new light coming in from these portals is here to assist the illumination of your DNA. These portals stream in frequencies of light through the grid. This grid is currently running around the globe very much like underground utility cables. It is bringing increased light to all the kingdoms, to your mineral kingdoms, and to your plant kingdoms. It is restoring the plant life, and as you are ingesting this new plant life, you are also absorbing this new increased quotient of light through photosynthesis and through the minerals on the Earth. Your waters are also receiving this increased light that's purifying the water for these spectrums of light can do this.

What is happening within the Earth is also happening within your physical body. The water within your body is being purified with the increased light spectrums streaming in. Your DNA is illuminating. Your blood is receiving the nourishment from the minerals that your plant life is bringing to you. This biological process that is occurring within your physical body is creating regeneration and rejuvenation. As your nervous system is receiving more frequencies of light, your physical body is becoming light. The radiance within when you close your eyes is becoming more bright, more brilliant.

Vortexes Support Your Body, Heart, and Mind to Hold More Light with Ease

The vortexes on the Earth Star are very much like the vortexes in your physical body. These are often referred to as *chakras*, but they are much, much more important and carry enormous amounts of energy. These chakras within the physical body line up with, and regulate glands within, the endocrine system. If you look at the gridlines on the Earth Star, and many can be found, you can locate many secondary chakras. They are in the form of sacred geometrical shapes that are formed when you connect them together. We would say that the grid line above the Earth Star is at your outer atmosphere. There is a team in light and a team in form that is working together bringing in more light, more frequency, and more sound, regenerating the full potency of these sacred geometric lines.

There are many different known grid lines, one is the Christ Grid that Jesus worked on when he was on the Earth Star. The Diamond Grace grid works in unison with the Christ Grid. The Christ Grid supports your consciousness and light, increasing the light quotient and connecting you to the higher mind of God. The Diamond Grace grid is a love grid connecting you to the higher heart of God. This mind and heart connection is the phase that the Earth Star is in now. It is supporting the Earth's ascension, and as an inhabitant upon the Earth Star, you too can ascend with her. These grids are here to support your system to step into these higher frequencies with ease and grace. These grids have been on the Earth Star since the beginning of her embodiment when she was created. You may have a conditioned belief about how long this planet, or your solar system has been in existence, and we want you to relax that belief to allow the consideration of what we are here to share.

All beings on the Earth Star have this same grid within them. It is part of your genetic makeup. It is part of your Divine creation, your Divine blueprint. The deactivation occurred as part of the fall from grace, millions of years ago. It was a major decision made by all of you to participate in this fall, all of you as a race, one race—the human race. Apparently, life was just too easy. You were connected to the divine mind through sacred communication with your soul. You were beautiful, healthy, and full of energy. You were true, pure perfection. You could do anything and create anything. You lived long fruitful lives and then, you reached a point, where you decided you needed to be challenged. You got together with the Council of Light (also known as the Cosmic Beings) who are responsible for deciding the future of the universe. They are the directors who influence matters of laws and covenants that keep everything in Divine Order. If a planetary race chooses to make decisions or an evolutionary shift on its own behalf, then it is brought to the Council for discussion and decision-making. The understanding was that you would eventually be able to reignite this grid yourself through embodiment after embodiment after embodiment, each time seeking the connection with the mind and the heart of your Divine Creator.

Up until now, there have been too many outside influences keeping that area, that aspect of your birthright dormant, turned off, or covered over. Humanity was taught to believe that divinity was outside of themselves, but this is not true. The Divine Child of the Divine Mother/Father, the divinity, is within you. It always has been. The truth of who you are is before you. It is within you. If you close your eyes and sit with this possibility that you have all that you need within, there could be an inner urge, an inner nudge to seek the truth, to know more about this Divine Light, this Divine Love that you have. Possessing an intense desire to know the truth is all that is required to create that initial spark, that initial spark within your internal heart.

There is an internal flame within your heart. Love, truth, and compassion for yourself help to fan that flame. There are images in some of your religious artwork that shows Jesus Christ or Mother Mary with their physical organ, the heart, on fire. They call it the sacred heart. This wasn't reserved only for them. This is for all of you. They were born in the flesh as well. They experienced this exact illumination that we are referring to. They were examples of what is possible.

Discover Your Internal Powers to Create Through Your Secondary Chakras

You may have these sensations of connectivity and increased frequencies emanating from your secondary chakras. Some of these energy centers are in your spine and are illuminating and bringing these spectrums of light to your spinal fluid. You are now becoming a Diamond Grace portal on the Earth Star. This is the portal for connecting to the mind and the heart of the Divine Creators or your universe.

You are made to be Divine Creator Beings. The secondary chakras of your eyes, ears, hands, and throat (breath and voice) are where you can create as well. These are vortexes where energy comes in and out. As you resurrect your Diamond Grace grid, these energy centers become even more powerful tools of creation. Your hands are how you create beautiful things. You may form a lump of clay at a potter's wheel that can be sculpted into something useful or beautiful, or you may pick up a musical instrument and play beautiful music.

Your eyes are connected with your optic nerve into your brain absorbing information. Pictures are stored within your brain. Your brain is like a computer with all these memory banks. As you increase the light quotient coming into your pineal gland and your inner sight, you can remove lower vibrational images or pictures stored within these memory banks. You can purify and cleanse anything you desire. Your eyes receive but they also give. You can emanate through your eyes. Be mindful of this as well.

It is known that your eyes can express your inner state. As this light quotient is expanding you are receiving codes, keys, and frequencies from your higher self and from the Diamond Grace portal. These can emanate out through your eyes which also helps to restore your surroundings. You can also give love and light—frequencies and vibrations—through your eyes. Increase your awareness of just how potent you are.

When you reach this level, when you recognize your Divine purpose, when you discover your internal powers, humility steps forward. As a being of grace, compassion and humility will govern these receptor sites, or portals, where energies can emit from you. We invite you to recalibrate your system on your own. Just gently let this integrate and allow grace to emanate from your eyes, mouth, heart, hands, and feet. Allow yourself to find grace within others. You are now in a state of essential harmlessness. You cannot cause harm or bring harm to any other individual. You are in a state of grace. We encourage you to spread that state of grace upon the Earth Star as you are called.

Use the Power of "I Am" for What You Desire

Your breath is a gift of the Divine Mother. You are breathing her love into your heart, into your lungs. She's giving you the gift of life. Your voice is where you bring all that you desire and require into your physical experience. You must be mindful of what you speak out loud. When you speak, there are vibrations and frequencies that emanate. These are attractors. Whatever you desire and require shall come into your life. Be very, very aware of those words beginning with "I am." This is the most powerful thing to say, for "I am" is the way of God. "I am" is you. You are the Divine spark of God. You are an "I am" being.

When you say "I am" followed by lower vibrational words, such as poor, ugly, or not worthy, you are creating that in your life. That is what you are reflecting. Your body is reflecting what you are saying. Your external experience is reflecting what you are saying. Instead, be inspired to speak what you want to have, be, and do. "I am a beautiful radiant being having a wonderful, amazing experience. I am a loving mother, father, child, spouse, or whatever. I am a generous and compassionate person. I am a wealthy individual with abundance in all areas of my life." What you speak sets in motion what will occur. The more light you have in your physical body, the faster the response.

Your ears are also points of access to this Diamond Grace portal or grid. Your ears are also vortexes. Be mindful of what you listen to as you are bringing this into your being. These words, sounds, frequencies, and vibrations are affecting your emotional state and emotions affect the physical body. Your eyes are vortexes. What enters your optic nerve is affecting your mental body, which can affect your emotions, which then affect the physical body. All is one. Be discerning of what you allow within these access points for all of it is affecting your inner landscape.

Rejuvenation Meditation: Purify Your Body with the Diamond Grace Grid

If you would like to clear out some of these lower vibrational things that have entered your ears or your eyes to your mind, or if you wish to clear words that have been spoken by you, you can ground to Mother Earth through the diamond below and ground up to the higher vibrational frequencies of the Diamond Grace grid above the Earth Star. Draw in those pure crystalline energies and frequencies of love and light. Ask to purify your physical body, your emotional body, and your mental body. Ask the light and the love to come in and bathe you with these purifying frequencies restoring your multi-body system to that of a state of grace. Ask these energies to clarify the power centers of creation of your eyes, ears, hands, breath, and voice and to align these vortexes within your body to Diamond Grace.

If you are just beginning this journey, you may wish to do this more often. Perhaps every morning as you lie in bed, or maybe while you are taking a lunch break, or as you go to bed at night in silence. You can reconnect to the Diamond Grace grid and restore the light and love quotient within your physical embodiment within your multidimensional bodies. This will assist you on your journey with ease and grace as you return to wholeness. If you stumble upon a boulder on your path, just draw this light from without and bring it within and speak your truth.

Say out loud, "I am a beautiful radiant Divine Being, and I am choosing to walk my path to grace with ease, love, and joy."

chapter three

Youthing and Physical Radiance

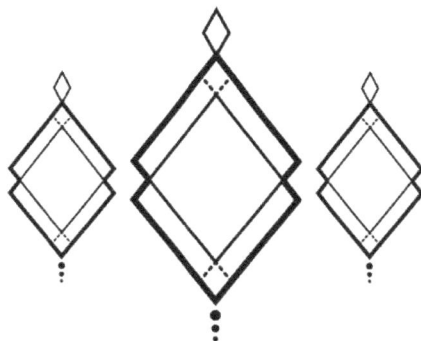

Creating Radiance Through the
Spoken Word

Diamond Grace is the Goddess of Cosmic Creation. As you journey through this book and create your inner Diamond Grace grid, you too become a Goddess or God of Cosmic Creation. These words are very, very potent. We are opening a wider bandwidth for you to receive. We would like you to engage in your own process of creating the Diamond Grace grid within your physical system. This will allow a more graceful connection to higher states of consciousness which are contained within the Diamond Grace portals that are all around the Earth Star.

Rejuvenation Meditation: Reconnect to a State of Grace Through Creation Words

To prepare for this chapter, which is about "youthing" and speaking your world into being using the vocabulary of creation, we would invite you to spend a few moments focused on this exercise.

Imagine that there are waves of Diamond Grace energy that enter through your third eye of the sixth chakra allowing in sensations of light. When you close your eyes, it is brighter within.

There's a warmness around your heart chakra. At first, it is just a sense of vastness like a void and as these energies are accumulating within your system, you may feel that you could sit in this emptiness forever. And so, the goal is to speak words of creation, to set the intention and momentum to amplify this experience. Choose to call out the creation words that speak your world into being. State out loud or within your mind's eye these words: *truth, love, compassion, restoration, rejuvenation, alignment.*

Now there is a warming sensation you may feel within your heart space and a shifting of the frequencies within your sixth chakra, the area where your pineal gland is located. This is subtle, so if you do not yet feel it, it does not mean it is not happening. It may feel like it is an expansion of inner sight like it's a connection of the mind, body, and soul. The soul is now becoming more expressive within your physical body. As the soul is expanding, it is reconnecting with the mind of God and to its original source of creation, the great central sun. This is the reconnection to a state of grace.

You have the ability within and through both intention and the use of your voice to raise the vibrations of the physical body; essentially, you have the power to restore the rate to its original frequency that was present when you were first seeded on the Earth Star. This feels very vast and yet light. There's no heaviness.

Have your heart be as light as a feather, the feather represents order, truth, and your heart. The sensation feels as if you are a balloon with gravity the only thing keeping you seated. Take some time to bask in these energies knowing that this has prepared your system to not only receive radiance and grace more easily but also to create your world into being.

The Power of Words to Create

Words are very powerful, and most humans do not know this, but words can create a life full of struggle, fear, and lack, and words can also create a beautiful harmonious life with abundance, ease, and joy. It's often heard that the universe responds to your spoken word, but your physical body also responds to the spoken word. It is part of the creation process. The cells are listening to you, and they must respond to your intentions. The truth is that we were created to live upon the surface of the Earth for as long as we desire in perfect bodies created by the Divine Creator, God, and Goddess. Through the spoken word, you can restore all the cells in the body. You can restore your DNA, filling the codons with more quotients of light. It is already there. It just simply dimmed down. The body knows how to heal scars, broken bones, and damaged organs, but *you* have forgotten. We are here to remind you of your power.

You were created with the innate intelligence to heal yourself. Acknowledge and speak the truth of this. "I am a Divine Creator Being, and I am the master of my physical body. I now call in the light, and I allow the light to enliven my physical organs, to rejuvenate my endocrine system, and restore all the hormones that should be released from all the sacred glands in my body." Revitalize all these sacred glands with love and nourishment from the light, love, and from your original Source.

Awareness opens the door and knowing you have been bombarded with environmental degeneration, with chemicals in the air, lower quality foods, depleted soils, and fear-based media, acknowledge how the stress of hormones took center stage within your physical body. Recognize that your body is not turning against you. It was simply protecting you from the external environment that was bombarding you to keep you separate from your truth. The truth is that you have rejuvenating hormones lying dormant within. If you could cease the excretions of the stress hormones, then there is space for the youthing hormones to start to produce.

You have been taught that aging is a natural part of life, so you expect to slow down, for your skin to sag, for your eyesight to wane, for your joints to hurt, and so on. We are here to remind you that those things do not *have* to happen simply because your time on this physical plane is in its fifth, sixth, seventh decades.

Speak about your desire to be youthful. Express your intent to have more vitality. This will bring your body into alignment with your truth. There are ways to limit stress hormones. There are ways to create calm and ease within the physical body such as listening to soft music, going out in nature, and engaging in activities such as yoga or tai chi. Some are going at a speed that feels like a hundred miles an hour down the road. Creating peaceful balance within allows these youthing hormones to come alive within your body, but it takes intention, practice, and patience.

Your Journey Back to Radiance

Your experience of the journey often depends on how broken or how out of alignment you are. For as long as it's taken your body to come out of the alignment, that reversal process can also take time and may often have a recurrence of some of the symptoms you experienced as you went out of alignment. For example, if it took forty years for your spine to lose the viscosity of the cartilage between vertebras, it could take that long for it to regrow, but each day is a day closer, so do not despair.

Do not lose focus as you journey back into wholeness! Embrace this pathway with the intention that you will succeed, for that is the way of the universe. It isn't like you will go to bed and wake up perfect the next morning. It is a journey back to radiance. When you speak your intentions and you keep your commitment to yourself, to your desires, the universe will bring assistance. These often will be a book, an article, a healing practitioner, or an alignment practitioner that comes your way. This is the gift of grace.

You will not be left out alone. You will have a team embodied and out of embodiment to assist you. When the body returns internally to a healthier state as the viruses and the bacteria in your body are removed, they are sometimes expressed as being sick, but you may have also heard it as a healing crisis. Just simply recognize that these are leaving your system. Think of what it's like to clear a drain, or a pipe, or a hose: The debris gets dislodged before it can be purged, creating a bit of clogging then sputtering before the flow is freed.

Affirmations: Joyful Journey to Wholeness

Take care of yourself and do not get discouraged. Instead, celebrate the departure of these unpreferred experiences. You can write on a piece of paper, "My journey back to wholeness will be filled with joy." You can put that under your pillow. You can carry it in your wallet. You can put it on your desk. "My reconnection to grace is my desire and my intention. I command that I return to wholeness with ease and grace." There are many words that you could use for your personal journey, and having a written reminder in front of you is a great way to keep your intention at the forefront of your day and give gratitude to all that are serving your journey to wholeness.

Rejuvenation Meditation: Mirror Gazing for Grace, Love, and Radiance

Be very mindful of what you think when you look at yourself in the mirror. What you think is what will appear before you. Everything vibrates, shifts, and adjusts based on your thoughts, emotions, and words.

When you get a chance, go to a mirror, look at it, and only see the beautiful parts of you. Show gratitude for your physical embodiment being a beautiful vessel that contains your soul. Do this frequently. It will slowly clear off the density that is shrouding your physical appearance. As you receive more light, this light can be captured by your cells and can begin to illuminate. You will notice your skin glowing and your eyes sparkling and the radiance, the radiance will be building and expanding and glowing within.

We invite you to gaze upon yourself with soft eyes and set aside the conditioned judgment of what is beautiful. We are pausing for a moment to infuse the frequencies of love into this section as you are infusing more love into your system while looking into the mirror. Gaze upon yourself with compassion, the same compassion you would for a small child where you see the beauty in everything they are, for you once were this small child. Without judgment, start with your eyes, look at your own eyes and feel the love from within. Send yourself the same love that you would for a child or beloved.

If this is a difficult exercise for you, then walk away or close your eyes and say, "I am beautiful. The beauty is in there, and I allow it to express itself." As you open your eyes and revisit this reflection exercise, be gentle and compassionate with yourself. The love of your Divine Creator is ever-present, and you are loved beyond what your human body can feel. Breathe in this truth, the truth that you are Divine, and you are loved. Allow the soul within you to look at yourself through your own eyes.

Affirmations: Speak Your Radiance into Being

We are bringing in some truth statements that will assist you in your return to radiance. You can create affirmation statements for yourself. Start with "I am," and choose beautiful words that you wish to see in the mirror. Here are some powerful truth statements using the vocabulary of creation. Combining these with the mirror exercise, and throughout your day is very powerful as you return to radiance.

"I am a beautiful, radiant, being of light. I am truth, and truth is beautiful. I am truth, and truth is compassion. I am truth, and truth is youthful. I am truth, and truth is kind. I am truth, and truth is wholeness. I am truth, and truth is grace. I am grace. I am a beautiful Radiant Rose Soul emanating beauty. I am radiance. I am light and love." Feel your body and the result of saying these statements.

Rejuvenation Meditation: Connect to Diamond Grace Through the Pineal Gland, Heart, and Navel

In this exercise, you are invited to connect the pineal gland, the heart, and your navel center, the area of the body that contains the gut and its deep primal intelligence. As the sacral chakra comes into alignment, you're reconnecting to higher intelligence. Remember that if you cannot feel this, you can imagine it happening. Some people have been conditioned to disconnect from the energies within the body or have been taught that this is impossible or difficult. Be patient with yourself.

Place your right hand on your heart, and your left hand on your sacral chakra under your belly button. Bring in light from the great central sun above, down through the pineal gland, connecting to the heart, and pause for a moment. Take a deep breath and with your out-breath, breathe this light down through your central column, or spine, and send it down through your feet to the center of the Earth, to the heart of Gaia.

Draw this light in with your breath back up into your heart space, and let it swirl in your heart space for a few moments, and then send that energy up back through your pineal gland to the central sun. Then with your in-breath, breathe this light back down into your heart space through your pineal gland, and then down into your sacral chakra. Gently confirm that you recognize this inner intelligence and that you are ready to receive the knowledge from within your own physical body.

Continue to allow this light to stream in, nourish, and awaken the dormant energies contained within. Bring this light back up into your heart space and acknowledge the increased radiance within your physical body. A deep out-breath brings that to completion and seals in this new light. Affirm that this is so. Even if you do not see it, speak it so. "My radiance within is bright, and I am allowing this radiance to express itself through the pores of my skin. My soul is perfect, it has been in a state of perfection within." It has not taken on the scars, the density, the hurtful words. It has been untouched by all of these, and it wants to express itself through your flesh. It wants its image to emanate from you. Allow this. Allow your soul to express its full image through your physical body.

The Diamond Grace grid will help raise the frequency and vibration of what's passing into your personal body. It raises the frequency of all that is absorbed by you so that it can no longer harm you. It can stop the degeneration process so that you can continue to be of this world, to mindfully choose foods that support and nourish the body, and still raise the frequency of those foods as well. The Diamond Grace grid has many spectrums of light and the color therapy within these spectrums can eradicate viruses and diseases within your physical body and without. It entrains whatever is absorbed by you to its higher vibrational frequencies.

Affirmations: Youth, Vitality, and Wellness

"I command and I demand that a Diamond Grace grid be resurrected within my own physical structure. The same grid that is on the physical Earth is now within my own physical body. I command the spectrums of light within the grid to express throughout my physical embodiment. I allow this light to protect me within this outer world. I am a radiant Diamond Grace Being of Light. I radiate youth, vitality, and wellness."

chapter four

Radiant Beauty

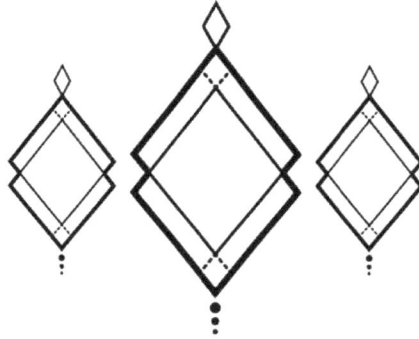

Embody Your Eternal Self

Radiant Beauty is a peaceful glow. It is the palpable energy of grace that radiates from your physical aura. It is often said, "She has the radiant air about her," or "He has this joyful personality or laughter. Everyone loves to be around that person." That is Radiant Beauty. This is a powerful message, and you may feel the emotions welling up. Those truth statements may be stirring emotions of wellness and a direct connection to Source. If you experience tears, they are tears of purity, like water, that can purify and cleanse.

Use the Power of Your Spoken Word to Reverse Aging

When you embody yourself fully you allow yourself to become beautiful. When you express the eternal you and bring that into full expression in this human embodiment, you are automatically resourced with all that is required to sustain the physical garment. This concept may be a little challenging if you are trying to grasp it with conventional wisdom, but if you choose to follow the understanding of your intuition, you will be able to sense the eternal you, as we do.

Now let's delve into the power of your eternal nature when combined with the spoken word to amplify your beauty and reverse aging. Metatron is coming forward with eternal nature to show that the power of the spoken word manifests whatever you speak. The vibration and frequency of those words create what is. Speaking the commands of your I AM presence is what you will become. Having your power words say, "I am eternal. I am immortal. I am beautiful. I am loving. I am passionate. I am compassionate," creates a frequency and vibration that resonates with immortality. They create a frequency and a resonance so that all the organs, amd the chemical/hormone production in the endocrine system within your physical body become a match to the vibration of eternal.

We also see eternal nature—nature as in what Mother Earth is providing for humanity and all the kingdoms on this planet—as all that is required to support the biological system being held on the firmament of her physical body. The herbs and the minerals, as well as the plants that contain a light source (it is an eternal light source held within these plants), were designed to keep the body in homeostasis (a balanced healthy state), to support your biological system, to maintain wellness. When you blend the two, the power of your spoken word and the bountiful harvest available upon the Earth Star, there is a synergy that occurs within your body. Within this synergy is a perfect balance of nutrition, light source, and Divine resonance from your spoken word which may suspend your physical body forever in whatever appearance you wish to create.

Restore Your Food and Body to Optimal Nourishment with Joy

The Tree of Life's qualities are radiance, joy, grace, and beauty. In the energetics of the physical body, those qualities are in the solar plexus. As you place your attention on this area, you may feel some energy radiating there. The solar plexus is governing the gut system, the digestive system, and the intake of food. This is where your gut instinct is, your gut feeling. You have a gut feeling or your gut gives you knowledge and wisdom. If this area is downtrodden, you may imagine that terrible things are going to happen, you may have a feeling that someone is going to say no, or you may feel that stress, doubt, and fear are running rampant in your life. All too often, these can be perceived as normal ways of speaking and thinking.

These thoughts and feelings can alter the quality and vibrations of your food, so it may not be as nurturing and supportive of your biological process. Instead, it is giving you exactly what it is that you're thinking. It's infusing your organs and your tissues with the lower-level frequencies and vibrations of what you think, express, and feel. Dr. Masaru Emoto conducted an experiment proving this. By simply aiming hateful or loving words at grains of rice over a period of thirty days, he transformed the appearance—hateful words created moldy rice, while the grains that received loving words stayed mostly white. Expressing peace, joy, grace, harmony, gratitude, and bliss while eating will then build momentum in the proliferation and rejuvenation of your cells. When participating in this mindful practice, your body feels worthy of being alive, radiating from within, and it starts to become an expression of joy itself.

You may now feel your brain lighting up all the way around. These frequencies and vibrations emanating joy and bliss are now coming up through the spinal column, through the neural pathways. You may imagine how the neurotransmitters spark and come alive with simply the thought of the joy of being who you are, as you express your signature source, your *beingness*.

You may experience new thoughts or feelings; you may feel a different purpose or a different reason for being alive. You're not just a person that goes through the days of the week getting up with an alarm clock, going to work, coming home, going to bed, then rinsing and repeating. You may feel that you are connected to a higher purpose, a higher reason for being alive on the planet in a physical embodiment.

Bring Peace and Harmony in to Shift Your External Appearance and the World

This may be a new way of thinking, but you are in command of your life stream, and this requires both focus and commitment. We are here to teach you that this was achieved in the way of being many millions of years ago. This was normal but throughout the eons of time, the quality of the atmosphere has shifted and is not as pure as it once was. The biosphere around the Earth Star has been absent of the full potency that would assist the human body to create this perfect homeostasis. There have been a few masters that have walked the Earth Star who were able to achieve this state of perfection. They did it with unwavering determination, intention, affirmations, and focus.

These same tools can assist you in maintaining a harmonious state in your physical internal landscape. Humans are waking up and acknowledging these truths. They are trying to rebirth the current biological state around the Earth Star. There is momentum going in this direction of bringing purity, peace, harmony, and joy to the lower atmosphere of this planet. You are assisting in this with your evolution by raising your own vibrations and frequencies. You emanate them out to those you walk amongst.

Bringing the same peace, harmony, and joy into your inner physical body may bring immediate shifts to your external appearance. As the stresses of the outer world dissipate, as you are no longer affected by them, that strain in your eyes goes away. The downtrodden smile begins to lift, and the twinkle in your eye is joy exuding outwards and is infectious, causing smiles upon others.

When you start to see the joy of life around you, your metabolic system will shift, and hormones start to secrete when you are in a state of peace and a state of joy. These hormones assist in the rejuvenation of the physical body. These are the hormones that you had when you were younger and full of vitality. There is no reason for these hormones to stop producing. There are elements and plants in your physical world that can assist your endocrine system in producing these hormones if you are unable to. Eventually, your body will know how to produce them again. It takes time.

Rejuvenation Meditation: Align Your Body with New Frequencies

Imagery can assist you in becoming the radiant beautiful life stream that you are. To begin this meditation, imagine a diamond with the word *radiance* contained within. Imagine placing that radiant-filled diamond in your solar plexus, which is the area where your liver, pancreas, and intestines are. Take a deep breath as this is overlying the area. The breath helps to open you to this powerful infusion of diamond radiance.

As you breathe out, imagine breathing out all the beliefs you currently hold that are no longer serving you. Watch those flow out with your breath. As they physically leave your body, thank them for giving you that experience and ask them to no longer return. As you do so, you are making space for more radiance to flow into this area of your body. Continue this cycle of breath seven times.

You may have a warming sensation in these organs, in your gut. These areas of your body are allowing radiance to infuse them. They are welcoming in this frequency and vibration. With these breaths, you may find yourself more centered and focused. Just follow your awareness. Express outwardly the qualities that you wish to be. For example, "I am joyful. I am peaceful. I live a harmonious life." Follow the energy that is occurring within. This is your body coming into alignment with these new frequencies that you are bringing into your life experience.

You may feel the palms of your hands heating up or you may feel the energy pulsing out of them. This is your electrical system coming online with these new states of being where you are now entering into resonance with peace and joy and harmony. You may feel the frequency or energy within your optic nerves as there is more light available to stream in. As you've cleared the density, you've made space for more light, more radiant light, to fill these now vacant spaces.

As you sit with this in this session, you can add more Divine qualities, or you can revisit this meditation and continue to let it build. As more light fills this radiant energy ball in your solar plexus, it can grow. It may expand beyond your physical body and out into your auric fields and even beyond that. It can radiate out for miles.

When you feel that you have come to a place of completion for this session, breathe in a deep grounding breath. Imagine your body is like a tree, and that you have roots. These roots are coming out of the soles of your feet and down to the firmament of the Earth. These roots are stabilizing you upon the Earth Star. As you open your eyes, remind yourself of the radiance within and the newfound stability that you have.

Continue your day in this radiant-filled body. Let this radiance express out of your eyes and your hands and share it with those around you. Share it with the plant and the animal kingdoms. Let this radiance be contagious. Know that you are loved and appreciated for increasing the radiant health of this Earth Star.

How to Shift Doubt to Confident Allowing

We recognize that breaking these cycles is challenging, but certainly not impossible. *Possible* is within the word *impossible*. We would invite you to imagine the word *impossible* to be "I'm possible" or to scratch off the first two letters and think about what is possible. "What is possible throughout this day? Is it possible to see where I made an impact on someone else's life? Is it possible that I experienced joy for just a moment? Is it possible that I shared laughter with my coworkers?"

Seek to find these little nuggets of change. Is it possible the other shoe won't drop? Is it possible that an opportunity may knock at your door? Is it possible that it takes a few years for the youthing process to kick in? You have many years of momentum for deterioration. Consider how it takes a little while to put the brakes on, slow to a stop, and then create the resonance to reverse when in a car, boat, or other vehicle. Perhaps it starts within and takes a few years to radiate out. Perhaps internally, you are now engaging the brake pedal that will eventually slow you enough to then switch gears. All these things are possible. You are the creator of your own life.

Our entire health system is built on the disease and the aging model. Another example is that we can see it's like trying to take your canoe up a two-hundred-foot waterfall, but perhaps there is another way up this waterfall. It isn't sitting in the canoe paddling. Perhaps you get out of that canoe, and you walk up the side of the waterfall on a clear pathway that has always been there. You circumvent the stream of consciousness that has been here for too long, that is steeped in the monetization of aging and disease.

This clear, easy path is simply the truth. The truth is you were created to have dominion on this planet. You were created to live a beautiful, eternal life. You were created to be a radiant Light Being with a physical garment known as the human body. These are simple truths, but to get to these truths you must take a different path than the norm. The body achieves what the mind believes.

We invite you to stay away from the word *belief* because in it is the word *lie*, as in the lies, the illusions. We invite you to seek the truth of your eternal nature. If you are an eternal radiant soul, then that is what you will become. We recognize that there is a lot of attention paid to the belief of deterioration and aging. This may require you to get to the point of stillness within meaning that your mortal mind has been accustomed to saying things like "we are all going to die sometime," or "as we get older." These have created an expectation. If that is your expectation, that will be the result.

We invite you to change those thoughts. Terri finds herself in a group of people who have these conversations all the time. She instead just smiles inwardly and says, "That's not for me. I'm choosing life. I'm choosing eternal radiance. I'm choosing to be on this Earth Star for a very long time." This change in your own expectations is like getting out of the canoe and walking on the clear path up the side of the waterfall.

About Aging and Dying from an Eternal Nature Perspective

Many people on the Earth are fighting the aging process in their physical bodies. There are many chemicals that they are injecting into their face to reverse the appearance of aging on their skin. This does not reverse the reason why these deep lines or wrinkles are appearing on their face. These lines and wrinkles are the result of internal feelings. Reverse the internal feelings and your appearance will show your current state. Radiate your eternal nature and notice your body begin to glow.

As your body glows and you embrace more of your eternal nature, you reclaim your power to live longer, which is what we are speaking about as the rites of passages of immortality which Diamond Grace helps with. So, what happens at the "end of your life"? Perhaps you come to a point in your journey where the physical garment is no longer required for your Earth Star experience. There is grace in that. Perhaps the life you've led has been too complicated or the evolution of your soul is ready for a different experience than living on the Earth Star. All is welcome in the outer physical plane. There is no right or wrong way to experience your life on this Earth. It is only your perception of it that makes it so.

There is nothing to fear when you transition out of your physical body. You're just returning to the light realms from which you came. All is choice, your choice, your conscious choice to stay on the Earth Star or not. We are just inviting you, if you wish to stay on the Earth Star, to have a life filled with joy and grace. We are offering you steps, tools, and keys to become a state of grace. Your journey in the evolution of consciousness is your journey and we acknowledge all it is that you wish to be and experience.

Reverse Your Current Dis-ease with Radiant Thoughts and Talk

You may ease your current conditions by acknowledging them. "I see you. I recognize you. Let's change. Let's go in a different direction." Perhaps it is pain; you can change your thought process or your perception of this pain. If you desire to release the pain, perhaps you'll be prompted to seek a practitioner that is skilled in that area. Perhaps it is a physical therapist or a chiropractor, or a surgeon, or whatever is optimal for you. Perhaps they are there to help bring you into alignment, to bring your body out of what is causing this pain.

Use that as rocket fuel and momentum to change your trajectory of this physical sensation. "I am on my path to recovery. I am on my path to rejuvenation. I am on my path to being well." If pain revisits your physical experience just acknowledge that you are perhaps feeling the pain of coming back into alignment. If you continue to see wrinkles on your face, acknowledge the

35

moments that you see yourself and say, "I look good today." Tell your body, "I know you're in there. I know my beauty is there. I allow it to express."

If there are days that perhaps you're wearing the strain or the weariness of a busy day just acknowledge, "I am allowing you to change. I am allowing the stress to fall away. I am allowing the beauty to express through me," and it will. It will be there. It is coming soon. Acknowledge the moments that you are beautiful always. Thank your body for expressing the beauty in that "now" moment. It's giving it permission to become that which you wish it to be.

Within the word *radiance*, is the word *dance*. Dance with these ideas. Dance with these words. Dance with these statements. Dance with the possibilities in your life. Dancing creates movement and can allow the light to flow more easily into your eternal structure and allow that which is stuck to be released. Dance with the possibility of becoming beautiful in all areas of your life. Dance with experiencing beauty in all areas of your life. Let the radiance of you shine.

chapter five

Divine Purpose, Superpowers, and Gifts

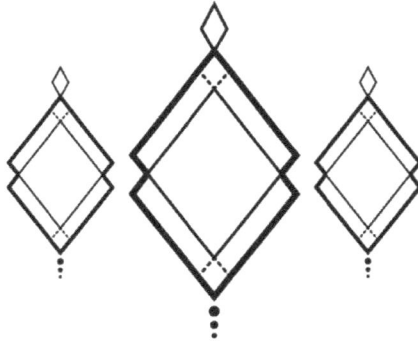

Amplify Your Soul's Purpose and Power

Your Unique Purpose Up-Levels Your System and the Earth Star

Divine purpose is your soul's ascended mastery. Divine purpose is your inner motivation to expand your consciousness in the ever-forward motion and evolutionary momentum. It's your inner urge, your reason for being a human on the Earth Star. You know you are expressing your Divine purpose when it brings you joy to engage in activities that are aligned with your purpose.

Purpose is unique to everyone. Many purposes involve community and connection with one another. It can be in partnership with Mother Nature and the kingdoms upon the Earth Star. It can be working with the elements on the Earth Star. Some Divine purposes include bringing off-planet energies, frequencies, and technologies to the Earth Star. Some purposes are bringing knowledge to the Earth Star in art, books, speaking, music, or songs. If any of these come naturally to you then you have a sense that this must be your Divine purpose.

If you are not finding resonance with what you are presently engaging in with work or community, you can try different modalities. You can explore different activities and see what brings you joy. You can reconnect with your higher self, your soul group, and ask to be shown your unique purpose or your unique gifts and talents. Working with your purpose helps everything on the Earth Star expand and evolve to higher conscious frequencies. It not only up-levels your system and dissolves lower vibrational energies and thought-forms, but it also up-levels every person on the Earth Star as your frequencies are emitting through the energetic waves surrounding the Earth.

Work and Career in Relation to Your Divine Purpose

If you have a career or a job or a source of income that supports your lifestyle and it does not seem to fulfill you, you can always find purpose outside of that container called work. It may be volunteering at a local community center, or teaching yoga, or being part of a community garden, or simply smiling at strangers. There are many ways that purpose can be expressed through you. You can explore other career paths within your career field. If you are an accountant and you went to school for this, perhaps assisting others with their financial resources is a Divine gift, but if it is creating chaos within your inner system perhaps you could explore other ways of using your Divine gift other than accounting.

There are many ways in addition or aside from your career to find joy in your life whether it's weekend activities or meeting a friend after work or for lunch or seeing an elderly family member and bringing a smile to their face. Do not underestimate the impact of your presence upon others in your community. This is very uplifting and nurturing for all. The elements upon the Earth respond to this joy.

Being joyful is very important to the biological system because when you are in a lower vibrational state, this is where disease can express itself. The feelings of joy dispel unpreferred experiences that could affect your system. Perhaps taking a walk in nature, going for a hike, or playing on a local baseball team could be what brings joy. Moving the body helps to dispel the energies and frequencies within your system so that there are no stuck lower vibrational energies.

Connecting to Your Divine Council and Soul Family

If you are not in alignment with your Divine purpose or find no meaning in your life, we invite you to go inward for a few moments while we guide you to seek your purpose for incarnating on this Earth Star. We can assist you to connect to your Divine Council, your soul group. If you are not aware of what your soul group is, it is a family of souls that are in the higher dimensional planes that typically embody together in some way upon the Earth Star embodiment after embodiment.

Your mother and father, for example, on the Earth Star in this lifetime might be your children in your next one. Your spouse in this lifetime may have been a grandfather in a previous lifetime. As you move out of embodiment, your soul moves back up into the higher dimensional planes for your soul never experiences death. Your soul is eternal.

You return to your soul family, and you review that recent lifetime and all of the knowledge you garnered. You, along with the Council, decide what type of experience you would like to have to evolve your soul's Divine purpose. Then you take embodiment again on the Earth Star in the physical form that best suits your purpose and your evolution in consciousness.

The I Am Race is from the same soul family. You are a Creator Race from the great central sun. Your purpose on Earth is to work collectively to raise the consciousness on the Earth Star, and to ascend to higher frequencies as a whole, to unify your consciousness, and to work in unison. In this example or truth, everyone you encounter is part of your Divine purpose and has meaning in your life.

Rejuvenation Meditation: Connect with Your Soul Purpose

Bring your awareness around your intention and desire to connect with your soul purpose. You can do this by sitting back and taking a few deep breaths to relax the body. Bring your awareness to your breath. Send an imaginary line, like an imaginary telephone line, up above and ask to meet your soul family or your soul group. Imagination works well here as you are creating a desire to reconnect, to be resourced with your original Source energy.

Take notice of what may appear within your subconscious mind. You may see a symbol, a sign, a face, or receive a hug from a loved one. You may simply notice flashes of light within your forehead. All is correct. All is well. Give yourself some space to receive and allow your sensations. When you feel you have received information or knowledge or insight, wiggle your toes and your fingers. Take another deep breath in, then let it out. Put the palms of your hands together and place them at your heart. Acknowledge that you have received the desired information.

Open your eyes and jot down a few words, ideas, feelings, or emotions. Take a walk in nature or stretch and just let it be absorbed. Do not put too much attention on the outcome. It may take a while to be expressed in your daily life. It may come through in a dream that brings more clarity. The important part is that you've set the intention and by doing so the answers, knowledge, or insights will come.

Dissolve Roadblocks and Align with Your Divine Mission

As you are on the path of expressing your soul's purpose, you may notice roadblocks or interference arising. Interference can manifest in many ways. It could be that your current family structure is chaotic and is suppressing your Divine expression, your Divine purpose. It could be a structural misalignment in your physical body. If you have a Divine desire (and we use the word *Divine* meaning extraordinary desire to express outwardly that which you know is your gift or talent), Divine desire will dissolve this roadblock on your journey to express your Divine mission, to be your fully amplified Divine design.

These family structures can heal, or they can shift and change. Your physical embodiment, the biological body, can shift and change and heal and come into alignment with your soul's Divine purpose. The cells of your body are under the command of your voice. Your auric field, the energy around your auric field, responds to the command of your voice, your inner desire. These shift the frequencies and light spectrums emitting from you. You begin to radiate and with increased light quotient, you are brighter. If there are darker energies or forces in your way, they will simply step aside.

Once you are in alignment with your Divine purpose, all comes into alignment with your mission and is there to support you. It is an unstoppable force fueled with desire and passion and nurtured with joy. You become more magnetic. Your biological system becomes more magnetic, and you will attract that which you desire into your life, into your career, into your leisure activities, and into your personal relationships. We are infusing these words and these pages with this energy of experiencing a blissful life.

Your Gifts, Talents, and Superpowers

You were originally created from the Divine spark of the Mother-Father God, the great central sun. You were originally created in the image and likeness of God. You had all your DNA strands fully illuminated. Each of these spectrums of light carries a gift or a power to utilize upon the Earth Star. You are in control of the elements. By your command, creation sprung forth. You recreated just as you were created.

Your biological body contains higher frequencies in the neurological system. When created, your chakras emanated these spectrums of light, and each had a unique power that assisted you to go about the Earth Star. You were able to create fire from your secondary chakras, a purifying flame. You were able to breathe underwater like a mermaid. You could walk on water like a hovercraft by the secondary chakras on your feet. You could create beautiful plant life that nurtured your biological system, that absorbed the photosynthesis of the sun and absorbed the elements of the Earth. You created animals for the sheer joy and beauty of their companionship.

All of these superpowers of creation and your ability to manifest or create are held dormant in the biological human bipedal now. You can reactivate your DNA. You can absorb the light to illuminate the dormant DNA strands. The strands of the DNA have different spectrums of light. These spectrums of light carry unique codes. The human population currently has two strands of DNA fully connected to Source, but what if all twelve were fully vibrating with color, sound, and information from the infinite mind of God. Can you imagine this for yourself? How would this impact your experience on the Earth Star? We invite you to be open and receptive to upgrading the light quotient in your DNA. You can restore your physical body to that which you originally were. Your soul knows how to do this. It is again, intention and desire that make it so.

Rejuvenation Meditation: DNA Light Spectrum Meditation

Rejuvenation is very simply done Dear One. It occurs in the light realms of your physical body. Light infuses your DNA, waking up or illuminating that which has been dimmed down because of old genetic patterning and mutated genes that have been replicating in a declining perpetual fashion. As you allow the light that is ever-present above and around you into your auric field, it is magnetically attracted to thoughts you are projecting and streaming into your vibrating physical embodiment.

Remember, you are really a Light Being, the elements and minerals are providing a structure for you to exist on this dimensional plane. The light is naturally ever-present and is there to nourish your true divine light nature. You can see the light rays emitted from the sun and the moon. These are there to feed your physical body.

Choose now to take a deep breath and go within, to the center of your heart, and into the original cell where your signature Source energy resides. Go within that space and tap into your infinite self. Connect above and beyond your physical body, connect to infinite oneness, to the divine mind of God. Imagine a spectrum of colors like the rainbow in the diamond shining light and ask the color representing the third strand to come streaming down through this connection. Breathe it in and let it integrate and infuse its light. Take a deep breath and then exhale.

When you are ready, go back up to the infinite mind of God, and reach for the fourth color and descend into your heart space. Infuse your fourth strand with this magnificent color from the divine realm. Watch these first four blend and dance in unity, a divine embrace. Take a deep breath, center yourself, from that heart space up through the crown chakra to the divine mind of God, and grab the fifth color. This beautiful spectrum of light descends back into your heart space and infuses your fifth strand with this divine connection, this frequency of light. Take a deep breath and let that integrate.

Then go back into your heart space and ascend into the divine mind of God and grab the sixth color in the spectrum and descend into the heart space to infuse your sixth strand. Breathe that in returning to the heart space and go immediately back up into Source the Divine Mind of God and grab the seventh. Drop back in and infuse the seventh with this colorful spectrum of light. Next, go from the heart center to the divine mind and grab the eighth. Feel the vibration of this eighth strand. Feel it pulsing against your fingertips; check with yourself and feel if you are ready to embrace this eighth strand. If you are, slowly bring it down into your heart space and infuse your eighth strand. This eighth strand represents the infinite potential of all that you are. Take a deep breath and embrace all eight strands communicating with one another pulsating with this light. This frequency of the infinite now merges and mixes with all the other colors. Let this integrate for a few more moments as your body enjoys the subtle return to its authentic self.

Next, come back to the center into the heart space and if you are curious, if you are ready, we will take you up to receive more. If that is a yes go with us on a journey up through your crown chakra to the infinite mind of God and grab the ninth strand. Feel the intensity of this color coming in and descending into your heart center. Watch yourself putting it into the ninth strand, and as you are upgrading to these higher dimensional frequencies you are more internal, and you are becoming interdimensional. Take a deep breath and recognize this as your truth.

Let us go back into the heart space and rise again into the infinite mind of God and grab the tenth color. This color will bring resonance with the divine mind of God, the Divine intelligence. The omnipotent mind, the Omni-intelligence. Pull it back into your system and back into your heart space and place this tenth color into the tenth strand and allow this spectrum of light to resonate with all the other colors. Take a deep breath.

Come back into your heart space, ascend once again up into the infinite mind of God, and ground the eleventh color in the spectrum. Watch it ignite at your fingertips and see how it quickly wants to jump into your heart space; place it into your eleventh strand. Allow this eleventh strand to ignite all that you have done; in all your embodiments, bring your potential back into wholeness. Bring it all into this lifetime and into all your embodiments.

Remember all that you have created and all that you have done as a human on the Earth Star. Come back into the center of your heart and with a deep breath go up through your crown chakra back into the divine mind of God and sit there for a moment with this divine intelligence, this divine peace. Then grab the twelfth color, and if you are ready, descend back into your heart space, and place this twelfth spectrum of light into the remaining strand. Take a deep breath and allow the divine infusion, the blissful joy of this reconnection to the perfection of the divine mind of God.

You are now in direct connection through these spectrums of light that are emanating a frequency and a sound that resonates with your truth, your authentic truth. You are in divine resonance with the all-knowing mind of God. Celebrate the bliss of your return to wholeness, your return to love. Feel these dynamic infusions resonate through the entire biological system and out through the energy centers of your physical body, illuminating your auric field with these twelve spectrums of light. You are the divine embodiment of Source. You are radiating pure love and light. Trust in the divine sequence of these spectrums of light.

Now return to your heart space, take a deep breath, and release it out. Breath that is within releases into your outer world and breath that is in your outer world merges within. Open your eyes and see the world from the eyes of Source. This is your new divine vision. Step out into your daily world as your newly resourced self. As you are ready, integrate your physical body expressing love, light, and joy on the Earth Star, delighting in the beauty and the grace of all the kingdoms around you. You are whole, you are love, you are light.

Divine Soul Purpose Emanating from the Resurrection of Diamond Grace

Resurrecting Diamond Grace within your system was modeled by the one upon your Earth Star many years ago, Jesus. Jesus restored the superpowers within his system, and he modeled this for the rest of us to do, and to know that we were also going to or have the ability to achieve these superpowers. It is written in the scriptures that he said, "Everything that I have done, you can do and more." It is written and recorded that he walked on water and that he healed people with his hands. He could turn water into wine. These are also your Divine birthrights, these superpowers. There are many examples in your written storybooks and in your movies of people embodying their superpowers and letting them flow. These are truths. These are Divine gifts and talents that are your birthright, and they are in your consciousness.

Modern Day Examples of Superpowers, Gifts, and Talents

Children are being born now with extraordinary capabilities. Young children can sing as if they were angels with beautiful angelic voices, or they can pick up an instrument and play as if they were Beethoven. There are those who can manifest instantly what it is that they wish to have in their lives.

Perhaps you are already expressing some of these superpowers. Perhaps you are wanting the perfect job and then your telephone rings and it is a job offer. These are examples of modern-day superpowers. These are just the tip of the iceberg. There are more coming, and they are modeled as your superhero characters.

Diamond Grace Superpowers

Diamond Grace superpowers may be frequencies emanating from your hands that can amplify perfection in your physical body. You may be able to hover your hands over an individual who is not feeling well, and you can energetically emit a Divine frequency of light that restores a particular organ into a state of perfection. Over time, you may be able to emit light out of your eyes that can restore the land, the Earth (such as a waste area), and you can transmute it. You can heal the water by touching the source, sticking your toes or your hands into a body of water, and restoring the water to crystalline pure.

Once fully activated, you may have the ability to touch the side of a silo that contains seed and restore the seed to its original Divine blueprint, where it is untouched by the chemicals that are destroying the Earth and all its biological systems. You can restore hope to another individual with a hug from the energy of love emanating from your heart. It will radiate and dissolve despair.

Grace is a Superpower

Grace allows all to be. Grace allows all individuals to be, live, do, and have the experience that they wish. Where all is perfect, all experiences have a purpose. There is no judgment. Grace does not force itself upon anything. Grace forgives for it is giving forward of itself and allows compassion to the darkest corners of our universe and understands its purpose. Often it is an act of compassion that raises the frequency of an individual who may be in the darkest despair and brings their own internal heart's desire to illuminate. The frequency of grace radiating over the Earth Star can fan this tiny flame. There is no expectation, however, it just gives. We're now infusing those words with the frequency and energy of Divine Love, love without expectations or limits.

Affirmations: Diamond Grace Affirmations to Amplify Soul Purpose

Here are some creation statements and affirmations to amplify your soul's purpose. We recommend you powerfully declare them out loud.

"I am embodying my Divine purpose, I appreciate my gifts and talents, and I allow them to be expressed through me. I am the resurrection and the life of the Diamond Grace grid expressed through my physical embodiment. I am the truth of my Divine Light Being expressing through me now. I am the physical embodiment of my eternal soul being. I am embodying my Divine mission. I am in alignment with the truth of who I am. I allow the truth to resonate with my beliefs. I allow any walls or roadblocks to disintegrate before me, to allow or reveal my purpose in this lifetime.

"I allow the guardians and the guides on the Earth Star that are here with me to assist me on my journey to find my soul's mission. I delight in expressing my gifts and talents for all upon the Earth Star to receive. I desire to connect with my soul family for clarity upon my mission and for resolution for my current experiences on this Earth Star whether they were perceived as good or bad, for there is neither good nor bad. All have a Divine purpose, and I acknowledge this truth within my heart. I radiate Diamond Grace through my body, mind, and emotions. I am radiance."

We would invite you to circle back and read through these again, and to also create your own statements that are bespoke to you and your journey back to Source.

Deepen into Your Soul's Purpose with Grace

Be patient with yourself and those around you. Be patient with your own biological system, for the momentum that you've created formerly is still in motion. You are now slowing down that motion and you are filling in your Divine blueprint with new colors, frequencies, spectrums, and desires, and it takes a while for the light to find form. Enjoy the process and acknowledge the small steps forward. Pick yourself up if you step or fall backward. It is all part of the journey. If there is a boulder in your path, acknowledge it, climb over the top, and keep going forward.

Your Divine mission is unique and bespoke only to you, and its expression outwardly will find its way in its uniqueness. It could be helpful to journal these experiences, to journal about your journey and acknowledge it on a deeper level. As you acknowledge it, you create momentum. Always, always give yourself grace.

chapter six

Money and Abundance

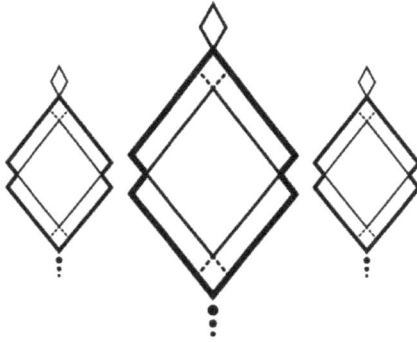

Rejuvenate the Crystalline Body to Magnetize Wealth and Wellness

A Message from Money: Rejuvenate the Crystalline Body for Wealth and Wellness

I, Money, am valued. There is value in the crystals and the elements of the Earth, the gold, the silver, the elements, and the precious gems. When you become crystalline, a diamond within your body, there is a value there, a value of Source abundance, abundance from above, the treasure chest above. You become an attractor like a magnet for the flow of abundance.

The Frequency of Gold, Silver, Diamonds, Sun, and Moon

Gold and silver also have a monetary value as you use them in this world to trade for goods and services. They are also required within your physical system for health and wellness; they appear in the form of colloidal silver and colloidal gold. These elements are used by the system to extract or repel viruses and bacteria while enhancing mental clarity and wellbeing. There is a wellness aspect to diamonds as well. You may imagine crystal clear water with the sun or moon shining upon it. The water sparkles like diamonds, representing clarity and purification.

The multi-facets within the diamond reflect the healing energies of the sun. These prisms of light heal the physical body and restore it to wholeness, the wellness that is desired within. It's like going to a spa that offers baths with light. Once you become crystalline within, you have your own source of rejuvenation. Much like a crystal that you can put out in the moonlight to restore and rejuvenate, you yourself can receive the same benefits of the silver from the moon.

The Goddess of Silver is coming forward to assist us in rejuvenating the crystalline body within your cells. We are infusing the pages, the words with the frequencies and vibrations of the moon. The light within is refracting these colors of the prism.

Sit back and relax with an open heart and an open mind and simply enjoy the frequency of silver. Joy is the key to allowing the flow of abundance to enter your physical body and into your outer world. When you feel that you are full of these nurturing prisms of light, slowly come back to center. Send gratitude and appreciation to the Goddess of Silver and to the celestial being that is the moon.

Rejuvenation Meditation: Sunset Meditation to Activate Rose Gold

This is Helios stepping forward and I am the God of your sun, the sun that lights the planet Earth. It is known that I offer nourishing vitamins. It is known that I assist the plants to grow that are harvested and consumed sustaining your life force with the vital nutrients that I provide. I have a twin flame and she is the Mother Vesta. She is represented by rose-pink energy. If you stare at my celestial body at sunset, if you stare at us with a soft gaze, you will absorb my golden light frequencies and as you maintain your gaze, you will notice rose-pink rays. These subtle rays are nurturing your physical body as well. They are nurturing your blood. It is purifying and it up-levels your vascular system.

We know that it is unsafe to stare at us directly during most of the hours of the day, but it is the sunset meditation where the light rays of the sun will enter the pupils of your eyes and nourish your pineal gland, your pituitary gland, your thyroid, and your heart. There is a chemical secretion that occurs that assists the endocrine system. There are hormones that are dormant within the human body that modern medical providers are still trying to figure out, and as these begin to secrete it causes rejuvenation within the physical body.

My celestial body energy has rejuvenation energy and frequencies. We are now offering these to your physical body to feel these fine frequencies streaming through your body. It is these light infusions that we are gifting to those on a mission to become a Diamond Grace body.

Gaia is sending an abundance of her frequencies and vibrations through the Diamond Grace grid, and it is connecting to you through the bottom of your feet and rising to connect with the Diamond Grace grid that's in your heart. Allow the expansion of these frequencies, colors, and vibrations to expand out of your physical body and into your auric field. Let this illumination simply be.

Have you noticed the renewed popularity of rose gold? The beautiful precious metal is used in jewelry, watches, and garments, worn to attract more abundance. We are streaming our frequencies into the rose gold now and divinely activating the precious metal. We are creating a Divine union. Rose gold represents the Divine union between the masculine and the feminine, the gold and the rose. This is assisting your own physical body to become balanced, a Divine reunion in this Rose Gold Sunset Activation.

Source Abundance is Yours

Source abundance is a gift from your creator. You are meant to have all that you desire and require when you embody onto the Earth Star. As your Source creator who is coming forth, you are born with everything you require on the Earth Star. Your Earth Star experience is to recreate in harmony, joy, and bliss. Whatever you want appears before you. It is a connection to me. If you are not experiencing this connection, you may be contracting and resisting, and you may just simply not be in alignment with me.

You can think of this abundance as a cosmic bank account. It is yours. You have the keys to unlock the bolt and let abundance reign over you and your outer world. You are all Divine Beings. You are all gods and goddesses, kings and queens. Everything in the universe is at your service. Step into this flow of abundance and ask. If you do not ask, it cannot come to you. You must speak it out. You must feel it within your heart, the deep desire. That is the way that it is attracted to you.

Be Mindful of Your Thoughts and Words to Stay Focused

Your spoken word is sacred. Be mindful of what you speak. If you speak about lack, that is what comes to you. It is the experience you will have. You are causing a contraction of your flow of abundance. You can choose at any time, and we suggest *all* times, to be in the flow and to speak of your abundance. We are inserting the word *patience*; the human is not yet adept at just snapping their fingers or waving a magic wand and the item of desire shows up.

In this world you are presently experiencing, there needs to be a flow of abundance, this is the necessary resource to purchase desired or required items. You must stay focused on your desire. You must stay focused and aware of your thoughts and words. If you open your bank account and the amount isn't there for what you require, try to address it from a different point of view to succeed in the evolution of abundance within your internal and external experiences. For instance, instead of saying "I do not have enough," you could say, "I'm getting closer. It's almost there, just a few more dollars," or something else that continues to draw forth abundance. The words help you stay focused on your intentions and your thoughts.

You can also set goals for dollar amounts. You can set goals for things you desire and require. Perhaps they are clippings of magazines, photos in a folder, or a Pinterest account of things you wish to have in your life. You can even have a little treasure chest of your own with photos, images, or paper money and coins representing wealth. This is known as an amplifier box. The items placed within are placeholders for what you want to fulfill.

There are other modalities and other Ascended Masters who speak of this. Abraham, as channeled by Esther Hicks, is one resource for learning more about manifesting your desires into the reality of your life.

Affirmations: Speak Abundance into Being

We invite you to go into some truth statements and create a vocabulary to speak abundance into being. "My physical vessel is where money flows in and out. I am an abundant being, a Divine Creator, and money flows to me and out. I give and I receive. I have all that I desire and require. I allow my bank account to be brimming with money, to be so full of money that I need to open another bank account. I have so much abundance that I willingly, freely, and lovingly give to those who do not have it. I have a blissful, joyful life and a closet full of clothes. I have beautiful bed linens and dishes. I have a car that I love to drive that starts every time I turn the key. I have all the resources required to travel."

Allow Wealth to be Garnered and Shift Your Perception of Debt

We are not suggesting that you be frivolous and wasteful. We are suggesting that you be mindful of your resources and allow the flow to come in, in a steady manner. Many on the Earth Star are not accustomed to wealth. We prefer the word *wealth* to the word *rich*. *Wealth* has a positive vibration and means different things to different people, but it always means security and safety. Wealth is a healthy lifestyle.

Rich is a beautiful word like if you are steeping in and rich with friendships or rich is a beautiful way to describe chocolate or like a saturation, but oftentimes the world *rich* also has a negative connotation, often associated with greed. Wealth is garnered. Wealth is mindfully achieved. Wealth is appreciated. Wealth expands upon itself. Rich can come and go, but wealth is here to stay.

There are healthy forms of debt as in a business transaction with a bank and a way to purchase a home, and then mindfully paying your monthly note, your I.O.U. back to the bank with interest. This is commerce, for the bank receives an income for lending the money to you to purchase a home. This home is a gift, a beautiful castle for you to reside in. The value of your home often increases. When you sell it, it's like a big windfall in your favor. Your home is kind of like a savings account. These are mindful ways of looking at words that may sound negative.

Shift Contraction to Creation

We will shift gears a little bit and speak about garnering wealth around your peers or family members who are not in the flow. You may be concerned about judgment, but this is part of the focus, staying in your lane, living your life to the fullest potential that you can envision for yourself. Oftentimes your peers or family members will follow your lead for you are the way-shower, an example.

Stay in your lane. Stay centered. Allow the light to flow in and trust in the Divine process of allowing. Once you go into the worry of comparison, you are in the contraction phase. When these sensations come into your mind or your heart recognizes them, allow the light to infuse with the truth and simply let go.

Just as the female body contractions begin to allow a baby to be birthed, contractions can be a way of opening. When you notice the contraction, breathe in the truth, breathe in your desires, and then let it expand and stay in that newly expanded state. If you feel a contraction again, feel that new expanded space with more light, more desire, more inspiration, and more love for yourself. The contraction may represent words like *not worthy* or *doubt*. Acknowledge the contraction, acknowledge that sensation, and acknowledge the word that's causing the contraction. Then relax and allow the flow to come in and feel into that new expanded space with more of what you desire to become.

Take deep breaths into your lungs. Consider that as you breathe in, you are opening, allowing flow as you expand the rib cage, and you contract as you exhale, shrinking back, getting rid of that which no longer serves: carbon dioxide, toxins, waste, negative words, doubts, and fears. Breathe in all that you desire and require. Then gather all the words that cause contractions and breathe them out. Eventually, your flow of input and output are a match.

Affirmations: Flip Contraction into Creation

If this is an area in your life where you are struggling, you could write all the things that are welling up within, all the things on one piece of paper that are contraction statements. "I don't have enough. I am not worthy. I am not loved. I have no value." Then on another page, you can write the exact opposite of those. "I am loved. I am worthy. I have value to bring to the world."

You can physically breathe in the words, the desire statements, the inspiration statements, the creation words. You can physically release the contraction statements by breathing those out. "I allow the feeling of unworthiness to go back into the wholeness through my breath, to be returned, to be resourced into the creation statement of I am worthy." Repeat this until all your contraction statements have been replaced with creation statements.

As the contraction statements have disappeared, so too remove them from your page. Erase them, shred the paper, or burn them. They are no longer required within your system. Keep your creation statements with you. Put them in your treasure box, your abundance box. The vibration of these creation statements has now been breathed into your lungs. The vibration of this is now flowing through your physical embodiment and are magnetic attractors for the very things you desire and require.

Affirmations: Diamond Grace Magnetic Attractor Wealth Statements

"I am a beautiful, Radiant Rose Soul. I am a youthful, Radiant Rose Soul. I am an abundant Radiant Rose Soul. I am a benevolent Radiant Rose Soul. I am a compassionate Radiant Rose Soul. I am a joyful Radiant Rose Soul. I am a magnetic attractor of all that I desire and require, and radiance exudes from within my physical body. I am a Diamond Grace Radiant Rose Soul."

We are grateful for these new frequencies, infusions, and concepts. It is our desire to reconnect with every soul embodied upon the Earth Star to go forth in grace and know they are loved. All is well. Be well.

chapter seven

Joy-Filled Living

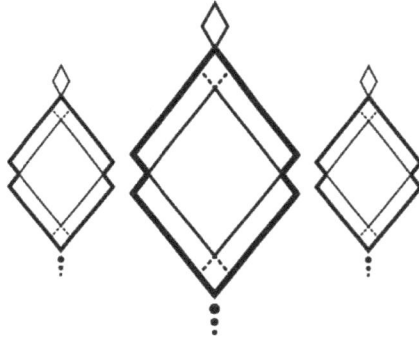

Radiance from Within

Archangel Haniel, Lady Radiant, Isis, Osiris, the Immortal Demeter, Immortal Aphrodite, Archangel Chamuel, Lord Metatron, and Lord Melchizedek are here assisting me in holding the space and scribing the information. We are delighted to come forth today with this group gathered in light. We love the topic of joy. Joy is the rocket fuel for resurrection. Joy is generated from within.

Internal Joy Changes Your Perception of Outer Experiences

Divine joy–extraordinary joy–is when your emotional body is radiating love from within. It is different from human joy where on a hot summer day ice cream can bring you joy, or when someone gives you a gift that can bring you joy. Those are external actions or activities that are temporarily based on your emotional body at that time. Divine internal joy is when your emotional body has absorbed the light and the love from the highest expression and is Source-filled with love and light. There comes the joy of knowing that you are Source, that you are a Divine Being having a human existence. There is the joy of reconnecting to your truth and to your higher purpose and understanding the reason for your embodiment on the Earth Star.

This internal joy changes the perspective of your outer experiences on the Earth Star. As you are internally joy-filled, you outwardly see and express joy to others, and you find that your normal daily activities bring you outward joy as well. When you are in Divine alignment with your highest expression of yourself, with your Divine purpose, and living a life joy-filled, this is bliss. It is absent of mundane emotions, lack, and lethargy. It's an inner drive to just be. It's an inner drive to engage with others, to express whatever your gifts and talents are, and this perpetuates more joy.

The state of joy and bliss creates a chemical reaction within your cellular body and alters cell growth, cell division, and cell health to create a healthier human form where disease cannot exist. This starts the rejuvenation process of your physical body. As you absorb more of this love and this light from the higher dimensions, it infuses with the biological process of your newly rejuvenated system and brings more radiance to the flesh structure.

The Diamond Grace grid is directly connected to galactic light. When you resurrect the grid within your personal system, it is automatically in communication with the Diamond Grace grid under your feet. It is bringing you galactic light, light that has not been on the Earth Star before. This unique light is filled with the nourishing spectrums of light that are up-leveling your DNA and removing unpreferred energy, lower vibration energies contained within your physical body and your auric field. It is like galactic light therapy.

Rejuvenation Meditation: Garner More Joy

To garner more joy, more cosmic joy, Divine joy, you can do this at any time in your life. Simply affirm within, "I am filled with Divine joy. I am resourced. I am connected to the joy from the higher dimensions. As I place my attention on the Diamond Grace within, I am resourcing my physical body with this joy, this unlimited joy. I radiate joy in all my outer activities. I find joy in all my now moments. I have a life that is full of bliss and satisfaction from performing my daily activities."

If this is too difficult and you still do not feel like you are being infused with more joy, follow these affirmations with this breathing exercise. Start by seeing and breathing the letters in the word *JOY*. Breathe in the *J*. Breathe in the *O*. Breathe in the *Y*. Breathe out words that are coming up like fear, lack, or hate. Breathe those out of the body. See the physical words float out into the wholeness and disappear. See the word *joy* come into your lungs. As you breathe out the unpreferred emotions, you create more space for the preferred emotions.

You can visualize the letters with beautiful iridescent bright colors. These beautiful radiant joy-filled colors will be absorbed by your lungs and infused in the oxygen in your breath. They are going in and nourishing all your organs and all your biological systems with these joy-filled spectrums of light infusing yourself from within. If you need further assistance, you can call upon Archangel Haniel who is the archangel of joy and grace.

As the cells divide and replicate, you are increasing these joy-filled cells within your body, and they are multiplying very quickly. As the older cells that are dying off and those that do not have this joy are removed from the physical body, you are slowly infusing your body with more joy. A higher quotient of joy-filled cells is nurturing, healing, and restoring your entire biological system. These joy-filled cells do not perish. They are fueled with a light source from higher dimensions. If they stay connected to this nourishing Divine light, they are eternal. When the human body has rejuvenated itself with these joy-filled cells, a Divine biological process occurs within the physical body.

Radiate Eternal Joy from Within to Change Your Environment

As the joy-filled cells are radiating from within your physical body, they radiate out of your energy system and your energy centers, otherwise known as chakras. Then they fill your auric field with this joy-filled light, and this is when your auric field starts to radiate. There are many paintings or illustrations of Ascended Masters that have this glow, this radiance about them. This is how it occurred. Your whole auric field is now radiating with this joy.

When everything is full you can express these out and onto the Earth Star. You can infuse all life on the Earth Star with this radiance, this joy, and bring about restoration to the outer world. You can bring restoration to your plants, to your water, to the animal kingdoms. This is a very necessary process for the future of the planet Earth. You are the Creator Race of this planet Earth, and it is your birthright to live on this Earth Star with all its beauty and wonder, and the time is now to purify this Earth Star just as you are purifying and radiating light within yourself, you will be restoring this planet as well.

If you are not expressing your fullest potential, or if you are not feeling joy in your daily life, it can often be expressed as tiredness, lethargy, and boredom. Maybe you have relationships that are always in constant struggle. Maybe your ego is always in the forefront causing conflict. As you absorb more of these light rays of joy, you shift your perspective. Light brings knowledge. Light is knowledge. Light is from the divine mind of God. It shifts your perspective to see from a higher perspective all your situations on the Earth Star. You become less judgmental and more grace filled.

This joy quotient increases within your system and shifts your perspective. You begin to enjoy, and you are in joy with the relationships around you. You become more accepting of others' beliefs and truths. You are creating joy within your environment. You go to the grocery store with a smile on your face. This joy is contagious, and it puts a smile on other people's faces. Your eyes light up and just saying "Hello. How are you?" shifts the experience of the one before you instantaneously. Exuding this joy changes the atmosphere within your own system, your own auric field, into your own home environment, and then into your town. As this joy radiates out, you are living in a more joy-filled environment.

Biodynamics of Joy and How They Affect Your Physical System

Your body is listening, and your body responds to your mental and emotional output. When you are stressed, your body produces cortisol. When you are in fear, your body produces adrenaline. Both have their place in the human experience, but an abundance of those is toxic to the biological system. If you continue to flood your body with these hormones, the body can slowly shut down with this toxic overload. As you increase the joy in your life, your internal experiences shift as well. There is no longer a need to produce or overproduce these other hormones. Instead, your body is listening.

The intelligence of your endocrine system and the intelligence of the glands will start to release these endorphins, more happy hormones. We are here to teach you that there are many, many, many hormones that have been dormant within your system. As you nourish your body with these rejuvenating hormones, these youthful hormones affect the biodynamic process of your physical body. Instead of internal destruction, you are creating internal resurrection, a reversal of this oxidative stress.

The human body naturally produces, for instance, CoQ-10 until a certain age, and then it slows down production, along with estrogen, testosterone, and progesterone. These come to a peak and then the natural biological process of slowing down and aging begins. This was the way that it was meant to be on the Earth Star for many, many, many years, but as it is time to restore the Earth Star it is also time to restore the youthing process or the natural homeostasis process of the physical embodiment. The decline within the cells is no longer necessary.

These rejuvenation and immortality hormones were turned off for the human body to transition, for the soul to leave the human body in the change called death and reincarnate to learn, to gain another human experience for the soul to evolve. That time is no longer necessary. The time to restore grace is now. You are the one that is responsible for this desire, for the biological process to be restored within your system. It's through intention and attention that this will occur.

Rejuvenation Meditation: Support Your Endocrine System

There are many sacred geometries and many spectrums of light that are all encoded with this information. You do not need to know them specifically. You just need to acknowledge the truth of this and create the desire to restore the process. These are inward intentions of your desire, and you must speak them or think them with the intensity or the level that you wish for this to occur within.

"I command and I demand that my endocrine system is fully functioning and turned on. I command and I demand that the light necessary to nurture this process streams into and around me. I place my intentions on the truth of this. I acknowledge that I am a youth-filled being upon the Earth Star. I choose foods and activities that nurture and support my endocrine system."

The intelligence of your physical body is aware of your emotions and your habits. When you are making the right choices to sustain the light in your human form, your body subtly responds. You may notice your spine straightening. Your body may be elongated to create space within the chakras. The energy from your sacral chakra, which is the center for creation, starts to release that energy up, through, and out. You may see an explosion of light within your physical body with your eyes closed. This is an internal radiance of light coming from that sacral chakra like a beautiful sunset orange. It is very subtle and gentle.

You may feel the secondary chakras in the palms of your hands and your feet start to emanate energy. This is the light radiating from within and expressing without. Let this light flow. You do not need to sit in quiet repose for the rest of your life to cultivate this emanation of light. Just simply acknowledge the process has begun and it will do it on its own. We encourage you to live your life as you wish and as you do, spreading this light to others is the Divine purpose.

As you do sit in meditation and receive energy and light from the Divine, you can open the palms of your hands upward and receive. If you connect to Mother Earth, into her heart chakra, the soles of your feet can connect to these chakras and absorb her love and her light, reconnecting you to the mother of your Earth Star. You can send waves of gratitude in return by reversing the palms of your hands to face the Earth and push love from your heart down to the center of the Earth. As you do, she will send back waves of love and gratitude filling your heart so full, reconnecting you to your purpose for embodying on the Earth Star and the Divine mission of restoring grace upon this Earth.

The innate intelligence of the human body knows how to restore. The body achieves what the mind believes. Hold this perfect vision of yourself within the center of your heart and the center of your mind, your brain. Hold your vision within and continue your intentions and affirmations for that which you desire and for your desired outcome.

We offer the advice to continue to seek assistance from professionals in the field of endocrinology or neuroscience. Also, we want you to call upon your guides and your angels. They cannot come unless you call upon them and their assistance is vast. It is their desire to assist you. They will flood your system with waves of energy that are the qualities of joy, vitality, love, and grace.

Eternal Joy to Restore the Telomeres

As these waves of joy radiate from within your physical body, this brings alignment to your hormones and regenerates your DNA. The ends of the DNA strands look like the ends of a shoelace that have a plastic tip on them to keep the fibers from fraying. These are the telomeres. Joy keeps these telomeres intact. There are also herbs like astragalus on the Earth Star to nourish your system and keep these telomeres intact. They are receptors of information.

If you break down the word, it starts with *T-E-L-E* like a telephone. These are necessary receptors that are filling your DNA with love and light and codes. Joy lets your body know to keep these intact and to halt the aging process. The lack of joy lets the body know that you do not enjoy your embodiment and that you want to transition out.

Rejuvenation Meditation: Expand Your Joy Leaps and Bounds

To integrate your enhanced state of joy we invite you to take a few moments to visualize your joy expanding in leaps and bounds. Visualize and experience joy as this geyser, an internal spring of joy that is rising through your chakra system, then coming out through the crown, and then cascading back down, being resourced and reabsorbed through the feet and then up again. Now that the joy is running fully in your system, imagine your life experience on Earth being like a beautiful body of water filled with lily pads.

As you go about your activities in more joy, you are leapfrogging to your next lily pad or experience. As you do, you leave your imprint of joy on one lily pad or experience and then you leap to the next and leave an imprint of joy there. Then you continue to hop to the next and you leave an imprint of joy there. This expands your joy-filled living by leaps and bounds and ripples out by modeling to others this grace and joy-filled way of living.

These joy lily pads are lighting up. As others jump on these lily pads, joy comes through their secondary chakras on their feet and hands. These energetic imprints are left for others to walk into. As you're leaping with joy you have no time to be depressed or angry. You're so happy that the lower vibrations cannot affect you. They're simply dissolving out of your experience and what remains is a joy-filled life radiating grace from within.

chapter eight

Radiant Alignment

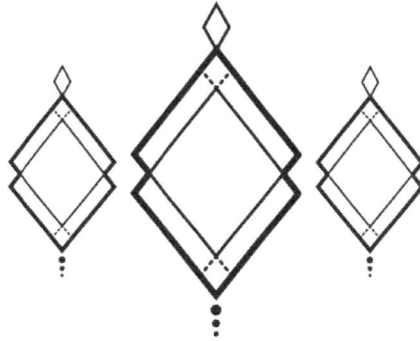

The Path of Grace

Dispel Distractions; Stay Focused and Peaceful

Achieving a state of grace while the world is evolving around you helps to polish that diamond within. Staying focused, centered, and compassionate about your personal state of consciousness will keep you steady, mindful, and well. In these times, there is turmoil on a global scale. There are many distractions that could pull you away from your personal desires to experience more grace in your life.

Taking a deep breath and focusing on the light within your pineal gland, staying in direct communication with the Divine, breathing in and out the breath of the Divine Feminine, and connecting consciously to the heart of the Earth will keep you stable while the outer world is continuing its drama.

When your inner state of beingness is calm and peaceful, it shifts your perspective and up-levels your wellness, so that the stress hormones cannot affect your physical body because they are not being produced. Your peaceful inner state instead causes joyful, peaceful hormones to secrete and take the place of the destruction in your physical body bringing rejuvenation and wellness to your physical garment.

Unify Your Mind with the Divine Mind and Act from Higher Consciousness

As you unify the Light Being with your physical flesh, your physical garment, and you've connected to the Christ Consciousness, you reconnect to higher intelligence. Christ Consciousness is unity consciousness. It is unifying your mind with the intelligence of the Divine Father. It's becoming one with the father, the male/masculine concept. You are all children of the Divine Masculine and the Divine Feminine. You are the Divine Child, the Divine Light.

You are a part of this world, but you are thinking and acting from a higher consciousness. Staying centered and focused on your own Divine purpose and your own experience of life in a physical garment, you are simplifying your inner state. It's as if you are sitting next to a serene lake and watching the world spin around you, but within your personal experience is peace and calm and joy. Your experience is outside of this world. Your experience is absent of fear, lack, and doubt. There's no division in your inner state of beingness. When you can reach this state of being, you are experiencing oneness.

You are experiencing the oneness of all life on this Earth Star and outside of this Earth Star. You've realized that planet Earth is one race, the human race. From this higher perspective, you can also feel and know that the life on other planets, other Light Beings in our solar system, are also desiring to work in unison as we are all part of one solar system. When you connect to the truth of your Christ Light, there is no longer a need to seek solace or advice in separation consciousness.

Many religions around this Earth Star are based on thinking you are separate from Christ, that only one person could achieve a resurrection. Jesus's life was to show us how to become a Christ. Jesus Christ was born Yeshua Ben Yosef (Yusuf), but he achieved the Christ Light within and became Jesus Christ. That light is now expanding within these pages, which makes this a wonderful time for light infusions of the Christ.

Rejuvenation Meditation: Perfecting Light to Ignite Your Diamond Grace Radiant Body

We are infusing the pituitary gland and the pineal gland with the light infusion of Christ so that you can come into fully aligned radiance. Now we are going to resurrect a geodesic dome within the solar plexus and then infuse that with light. Grounding the light within your solar plexus is the resurrection of grace. Grounding the Divine Masculine in the mind and the Divine Feminine in the heart and streaming the light through both of those ignites grace within the solar plexus.

The solar plexus is the power generator. It is where the radiance of your internal light is housed. As you bring in the Diamond Grace grid within your physical embodiment and you connect the love of the Divine Mother within your heart, the light, love, frequencies, vibrations, or sacred geometry is within, over your heart center.

Envision the vertical light and the horizontal light replicating the cross. The horizontal (like a person holding arms out, even with shoulders) is love and the vertical (up and down skull/spine/legs) is light. Those two come together in resurrecting the radiant body. It's that unification of love and light that creates the grace body and the radiance within, and the solar plexus is the energy center or the radiance that maintains or powers it. You may be experiencing many sensations at this point. There may be an expansion of light in the midbrain area and a swirling of light around the heart chakra. You might feel that light energy circulating throughout the entire chest cavity. In the solar plexus, there is a beautiful warm heat and with every breath, an expansion of all three of those areas. Notice the secondary chakras in the palms of your hands and your fingertips. They may be emanating a radiance, a light, or a frequency. This light is a perfecting light. It is permeating the atmosphere, the space, the air, and all the elements.

It's transforming everything into a state of perfection. Now it is really radiating more light and keeping you connected to the higher dimensional frequencies above. You may feel the light streaming in through your crown chakra. Breathe in the breath of the Divine. It is now building momentum. These streams of light are nourishing your pituitary, your pineal gland, and your hypothalamus, increasing your intuition and your inner sight. The Christ body is contained within the pituitary gland. You may experience flashes of light as things are expanding. Neural networks are being rewired and resourced. Enjoy and allow this upgrade within your system. Acknowledge the sun and the moon for their Divine intervention in your life. Give thanks and appreciation to yourself for being an active participant in the restoration of grace and the human body currently in the Earth Star experience. As you give gratitude, waves of gratitude return from the Divine. Allow these waves of love to wash over your physical body and amplify the joy within. The word *allow* is coming through. Allow this Divine transformation to express your outer experiences. View the environment around you with the eyes of your Light Being, your soul, looking out through your eyes.

You Are Honored for Fulfilling Your Divine Purpose

You have now become a portal of Diamond Grace. This is the resurrection of the Diamond Grace body. You have achieved the journey back to grace. Your new journey has just begun as becoming Diamond Grace on the Earth Star, creating with purpose in a state of grace. As a Diamond Grace portal, you are a receiver for Grace Codes.

You are the connection for Divine Grace to stream from the higher dimensions into the grid around the Earth Star. You are assisting the evolution of the planet Earth with these Divine Codes infusing the lower atmosphere of Earth, the firmament of the Earth, and all life upon the Earth. You are restoring the soils and the waters, the air elements. This contribution to the Earth Star is the most benevolent thing a human can do.

Bring grace to the wind, the rain, and the oceans, and diffuse the anger contained within these elements that have caused destruction to humanity. Consciousness is held within the elements of your Earth Star. These lower consciousness frequencies, thoughts, and vibrations have been causing your mega-storms. Infusing these elements with the Grace Codes is bringing grace to all upon this Earth and to the biological process of this world, the physiological atmospheric conditions within the Earth, and above the Earth.

Your contribution is grand, and you are honored for your role in the purification of this planet and all those who reside upon it. As you are now a portal for Diamond Grace, you are walking in grace, with grace, and as grace. This is fulfilling your Divine Purpose. There are a lot of codes streaming into the pages at this moment. They are coming to you like a silent Light Language.

The perfecting light is from pure Source energy. It does not have distorted frequencies within it. Your electronic magnetic frequencies currently on the Earth Star are infused with harmful frequencies that are causing destruction within your cellular biological garments. The electronic magnetic frequencies on the

Earth Star are causing cellular mutations within life on the Earth Star.

As you are emanating this pure Source light from the Divine, it is purifying these frequencies. The diamond is erected as an image around you. The light from the sun shines in, and many prisms of healing light, like healing colors, are emanating like color therapy. These different spectrums of light heal the physical body and purify water, eliminating the bacteria.

You're in unison with your Divine Light Being. You do not need the sustenance of the outer world, the physical environment. Sovereignty is your uniqueness. The quantum biodynamics of Diamond Grace is like a hot air balloon. The propane flame is its power source and its way to levitate and float away. It's like the light within reaching out and bringing radiance to others.

Rejuvenation Meditation: Quickly Tap into a Peaceful State

Create a peaceful, tranquil state within, and imagine that you are inside a diamond. Focus on the Divine light above and draw that through your crown chakra into the top of the diamond into your solar plexus. Feel this warmth within your solar plexus. Imagination is the beginning. Attention and intention create momentum. When it begins to feel real, you know you have achieved the radiance within. These are simple exercises and simple intentions. A return to grace is simplistic.

Perhaps the only challenge is to let the outer distractions simply fall away. You are naturally a graceful being. It's already within you. You are just allowing it to be resurrected within and to resurface. This a simple exercise to remember this original state of being is all that is required. It is a Divine remembering that you are already in a state of perfection. It is the distractions keeping you away from this knowing. We have purposely been simplistic in our words, descriptions, and exercises because it is not an arduous journey. It's simply an allowance to be, to return to that which you are.

Your Guides Are Walking with You as You Seek Truth in Your Journey

Truth is a doorway to your infinite potential. Your inner truth is seeking to guide you to the infinite potential of your life. Once you begin your journey in alignment, with truth as your guide, assistance will drop in, in more now moments. Synchronicity and assistance will be at the forefront of your life. Perhaps a suggestion from a friend or a pop-up on social media, or a discovery on your internet searches will light the way. These are beacons to find your true north. The path is not hidden. It has just been covered over.

Your guides are here to light the pathway for you, to seek the truth of who you are, and to help provide the solace and comfort needed on this journey to wholeness. Take the hand of your Divine guides and enjoy the journey to light with ease and grace and joyful discoveries of what you have been seeking in your life. The pages in this book are designed to infuse your journey with light and love as you return yourself to the state of grace that is within. I have never left you. I am Diamond Grace. I will personally walk with you as you increase the radiance within.

There are many distractions in the outer world that have the potential to keep you away from your Divine purpose. There will be many people in your life, in your workplace, and in your family relationships that will be affected by the ongoing commotions in their world and their consciousness; you can be a space of grace for them. Allow them to release those unpreferred energies in whatever way that is for them without reacting. Stay calm, centered, and loving. Be a sounding board for them to work through their personal issues at hand. This is being graceful in all moments. As the radiance builds within, let that radiate out into the world. This radiance is bringing peace to those around you. It's like bugs going to the light. Those around you will be attracted to your inner presence and to the love and the grace, the patience, and the calmness that you will exude instantly affects the atmosphere around you. It brings more peace and stability to the outer environment of those in your presence.

chapter nine

Reconnect with Source

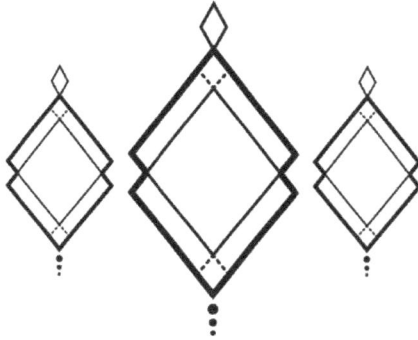

Regenerate Your Body and Home

You were initially created as the I AM Creator Race and was connected to Source. You were in a state of perfection and the electronic field around you was a protective mechanism that allowed you to live eternally. You had the ability to create anything in your life you wished to experience. When it was decided as a part of the fall from grace experience to disconnect this light, your connection to Source, you became the sole architect of your own life on Earth. As this connection was cut off, the grounding of light from above which is grace, the grace of God, was also severed. As you have disconnected yourselves, you are in control of your own environments, your communities, and your families without being resourced from the light above.

Many incidents occurred in the last several million years that have caused humans to experience deterioration and degeneration within the physical body and environments and have transmuted love and light into fear and doubt. As you are still the Creator Race, these thought-forms are still controlling your external environment. You are in control of the air and water elements, of earth and of fire. There is much evidence that humans—you—have long forgotten connection to Source.

We are here now to assist you in reconnecting to Source. You are still sovereign, free will, creator beings. You have dominion on this planet but becoming in a state of grace once again can allow you to experience life on this Earth in pure light and love. Restoring the Earth Star and your external environment would be very beneficial to balancing the ecological system, the plant kingdom, the animal kingdom, and your own physical bodies. Life is indeed extinguishing because of the lack of light.

The desire of the Mother/Father God and the great Divine Beings in the cosmic universe is to have Earth be the magnificent planet that she was created to be. You are stewards of this beautiful planet. We are inviting you to reconnect with Source and to restore all life upon the Earth Star, to rejuvenate your soils, waters, plant kingdom, and your physical selves. You are all interconnected as one. Your energies work symbiotically.

Transmute Your Home Environment with Diamond Grace

Your soul has the physical garment as a home on the Earth Star, and your physical garment has a home as well that has a roof and walls. This environment can also be filled with Diamond Grace light, energy, frequencies, and codes. You can transmute your home environment also. Your home environment has been receiving maleficent electromagnetic frequencies from the outer world via your telephones, TVs, Wi-Fi, internet, and possibly those outside of you visiting your home or living within your home.

You can transmute these energies by calling in the frequencies, codes, and the sacred geometries of Diamond Grace to anchor into your home environment and expand across your land, your community. You do not have to know exactly how this occurs or what the keys, codes, and sacred geometries are for this to work. It is simply by your asking that we will respond, and we will instantaneously connect with you and illuminate your personal space and all that you desire and require in every now moment.

Rejuvenation Meditation: Connect Your Home to Diamond Grace

Sit in stillness for a while and clear out all the distractions of the outer world. Think on or externally speak your desire to connect your home to Diamond Grace. We realize you may be in a place that does not allow you to speak your intentions out loud, but a strong internal desire creates the same frequency. Call upon the sacred geometry of Diamond Grace to anchor into your home space and imagine a glowing rose-pink energy funneling into wherever you are directing it. You are creating a portal from the higher octaves down into your home space and calling in all unpreferred energies to flow into this portal and allow it to be transmuted with the keys and codes from the Diamond Grace field above.

As you and your home receive these frequencies, unpreferred energies transmute into pure diamond white light. Allow this process to occur as you settle more deeply into your home space. Everything in your external environment is now resourced. The density of the outer world coming in through radio towers, transmitters, receivers, and wireless apparatuses are now diffusing with the Diamond Grace sacred architecture in your home. Any harmful frequencies can no longer cause destruction within your internal and external environment.

When you are accustomed to doing this, you can expand the

width of your Diamond Grace portal or vortex. You can call this portal remotely to other loved ones or geographical locations upon the Earth Star in alignment with their free will and conscious choice to receive it. You are a creator being resourced by God. It is your Divine birthright to bring grace upon the Earth Star in all its kingdoms once again.

Affirmation: Fill Your Home with Diamond Grace Peace

"My home is filled with love, light, peace, and joy. Fill every aspect of my home and my life. The density of the outer world cannot penetrate this space that I reside in. Nothing out of alignment for me, those who reside here, my home, and the land from the outer world may come through these doors. This sacred space is permanent and filled with angelic beings of Diamond Grace that are assisting all those within my home environment to be held within a state of grace, resourced, and connected in all now moments. So be it, and so it is."

Your Environment will Change as You Invite Grace and Peace In

The energy of Diamond Grace in your home may inspire rejuvenation, regeneration, transformation, transmutation, remodels, beautifying, simplifying, or decluttering. When your brain structure is decluttered from these electronic frequencies that have been bombarding it, as your food is purified by these sacred geometries and radiant light, more clarity comes into your thoughts, body, mind, and emotions. As you receive more clarity you begin to view your external environment with a clear field. As you declutter your body, mind, and emotions, you will naturally want your external environment to mirror that which is internal.

You may find yourself cleaning out your closets. You may find yourself choosing different colors. Colors carry sacred frequencies within themselves and as your frequencies raise with higher vibrations, you'll want to surround yourself with higher vibrations and frequencies. It may be decorations, clothing, music, relationships, or food choices. You may notice the plant kingdom within your residence, your home has brighter blossoms. The trees are healthier and happier as they are now reconnected to Source as well. These may all be a result of your clarification of being in the clear field, of your conscious choice to live in a state of grace.

For example, Terri used to love red and green accents in her home. Now she prefers lots of blue. Blue is supporting her now in her quest for truth, to search for truth, and to speak the truth. Not that red and green are less desirable as they were on purpose at that time in her evolution. As you evolve you may choose different foods to ingest for the frequencies of these colors contained within the food and the color spectrum of the materials that make up your pillows and furniture. They are emitting frequencies that your body is absorbing and assisting with the transfiguring of your internal and external personal space.

Align with Your True Physical Self

Coming into alignment not only benefits your physical home but your soul's home—the body. As you come into alignment and absorb more units of consciousness, which is Source, it naturally transmutes the lower vibrational frequencies which can, for example, appear as weight gain from a lower vibrational frequency of anxiety or degeneration of the human body and lack of hormones. As the hormones decline, the human physical body adds fat to replace these hormones that are diminishing. As your internal glands regenerate and rejuvenate, so do the hormones. These are the hormones that you had as a youth. These helped you with your youthful appearance in your vitality.

If you wish to accelerate this process, movement assists your intake of oxygen and your increase of blood flow which further nourishes your biological body. These help with the excretion of hormones in your brain structure thereby increasing these feelings of joy and bliss which dissolve and transmute anxiety and depression. These are your conscious choices. You are now in the driver's seat if you are aware that you are a conscious creator being. You are consciously creating your internal and external environment.

Movement and nature accelerate this process and help you to commune with your external environment and increase your awareness that you are all one in this ecosystem of your biodynamic Earth Star. As you resonate the higher frequencies, you are transmuting and radiating the lower frequencies, evolving and up-leveling the kingdoms you come in contact with. Get out of your dark basements and let the radiance of you shine brightly for all to experience.

Regeneration, Rejuvenation, and Transformation of Cells for a Youthful Body

In the human biological form, cells multiply. A discordant cell can multiply and create more discordant cells and perhaps create an unpreferred mass in the body or deterioration of the physical body–aging. Regeneration is a cell in a state of perfection multiplied and creating or stabilizing a healthy biological environment within the physical body. It is replacing the cells that were dying and aging and regenerating cells that take the place that are more youthful or healthy.

As these cells multiply, the appearance of the body may look more youthful or healthy because there is a healthier blood flow. As the organs of the body are regenerating youthful healthy cells, you are restoring the state of wellness of the internal and external environment of the physical garment, allowing oxygen to penetrate the furthest regions of the body with a healthy vascular and nervous system. The brain can communicate. The blood can flow. The oxygen can be delivered.

Transmutation, transformation, and *transfiguration* are also terms used in alchemy where you are transmuting the cells that are replicating in a state of imperfection and you are transmuting those cells into a state of wellness and perfection. You are transfiguring the physical body from within. Transmutation occurs with the light coming in, increasing the light within the flesh structure. This light is within the chakras. The chakra colors become clearer and more vibrant. These are truly sacred energy centers that can bring a holistic state of wellness to the physical organs within those sacred centers.

As you are resourced with this light from above and as you move into deeper and deeper alignment, any unpreferred energy from your external environment cannot infuse them any longer. As this light bathes you internally, it is also bathing you externally with a golden luminosity that creates a shield or a blanket of protection, a multifaceted field of Diamond-like strength radiating grace. When you reconnect to Source, all the cells in the body are ignited with codes. It's very simple; this is the way the human body was designed. If you stay in this correct alignment you are resourced with this nourishing light continually.

Rejuvenation Meditation: Reconnect with Source to Rejuvenate Your Cells

There is a connection and a hookup to the Diamond Grace galaxy to support this meditation that has not ever unfolded before. We are infusing this meditation with frequencies that will envelop you in a renewed, dynamic way. This infusion is occurring through an eye transmission with the author's eyes imbuing the words on the page with energy from the Diamond Grace galaxy. As you receive these words and energies through your own eyes, you may notice the frequencies are fine and refined like silk threads. You may feel your brain expanding and the neurotransmitters in your brain reconnecting and aligning with Source. As you deepen into this meditation, we invite you to pay particular attention to receiving supportive energies to reconnect with Source through your eyes.

Take a moment to connect to your inner state of grace and amplify your desire and choice to reconnect with Source. Know that this process is simple and guided by your intention. As your system aligns with your natural connection with Source, visualize a direct rod or current, a direct connection from Source energy cascading through the center of the brain down into the heart and through, down to the root chakra. This energy is recycled up through the spinal column and down and then flows out through the central nervous system. It's like an electronic frequency that speaks to all the cells in the body to instantly fire up and illuminate with the information needed to become a state of perfection which will cause them to regenerate to the original Divine blueprint. It will turn back the effects of time on the physical body. Notice the rejuvenation occurring, which will continue after this meditation completes.

You may be receiving information through the palms of your hands, and you may feel like your hands are pure light. As these newly resourced cells begin to multiply, they will multiply in a state of perfection, and any cells not in alignment with this newly resourced light will simply be removed by the natural biological process of the cell turnover like skin sloughing off and allowing new luminosity or the radiance of you to be uncovered. Reclaim your reconnection with Source and know that it has occurred through this meditation. Take a few breaths to allow your sensations.

We, the Diamond Grace galaxy came forward today in this meditation to create a powerful container that is within the pages of this book. Whether on physical paper or in electronic format, these words truly radiate with Diamond Grace codes. We have never been on the Earth Star in this capacity before. We are now in direct communication with you and the Diamond Grace portal is infusing our light in the most graceful delicate way. It has been the author's life work to build the portal for us to connect with. You also have been clearing the way and anchoring in the electronic frequencies required for us to stream our light. We are available to support you in your regeneration, rejuvenation, and transformation journey. You may simply call upon us at any time, and we will amplify the energy of Diamond Grace that resides within your system and your alignment with Source.

You still have the memory of being disconnected from Source during the Fall from Grace and you also have free will to connect and align or disconnect and come out of alignment with Source.

Affirmation: Anchor Diamond Grace into Your World

We invite you to anchor and ground the frequencies of Diamond Grace within you and in your home environment. You can simply state, "As a creator being I am choosing Diamond Grace in all my now moments in my internal world and my external world. I allow the frequencies, codes, and vibrations of Diamond Grace to connect me to Source. I am anchoring my alignment with Source and Diamond Grace from above my crown chakras through my spinal cord and down to the bottom of my feet to the center of the Earth. I am grounded. I am connected. I am resourced. I am in a state of grace. So be it, and so it is."

chapter ten

Grace in Nature

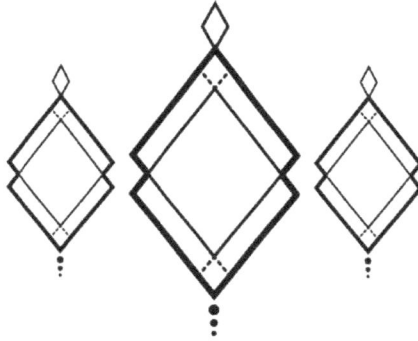

Manifest Heaven on Earth Through Serenity

Living in a state of Diamond Grace infuses all now moments for yourself and others around you with peace and serenity. It allows you to enjoy all the experiences of the outer world like a smile from a loved one, a hug from a friend, gazing outside at the beautiful trees, going in nature, taking in the beauty cf a flower, or listening to the melody of the songbird in the tree. Observe the seasons while being present in the space of grace that you reside, the smell of a fresh blossom from a fruit tree, the spring green of a budding leaf, and the deep hues rich with nutrients in the summer sun.

Rejuvenation Meditation: Recalibrate to the Cycles of Nature

As you journey through the seasons in this rejuvenation meditation, you'll attune your inner being with the cycles of nature to reset your system to grace as natural, as a given in all moments. Take four slow breaths to signal to your body your intention to receive support from the Earth, nature, and the seasons to return to your natural state of grace as a way of being in your daily life.

As autumn and the fall equinox sets upon your hemisphere, the fruits and vegetables are juicy and plump with nutrients for your physical body. The sun is in the sky for fewer hours of the day and the colors of the leaves are turning crimson, orange, yellow, gold, and red. It is a time for you to gather and nourish your own inner landscape with the bounty of life. As you transition into the winter solstice, it is a time to reflect within, to build your light within.

Reconnect to the vast cosmic universe above and allow the light from the great cosmic sun, the stars, and the moon to support you in the darker days of the night sky in the winter months. If you reside in an area where there is snow, take in the purity of the snow as it purifies and cleanses the atmosphere, the beauty of this crystal and bright white as the sun reflects off the snow. Play in this environment. Go out and embrace it. Express your love and gratitude for the water, the crystalline water that has become a snowflake or an ice-covered pond. This crystalline water holds the frequencies that you are emanating. These frequencies are now qualified with grace, your Diamond Grace.

As the spring comes, and the warmer climate melts this crystalline water, your Diamond Grace energy remains with this water element wherever it may flow. This flow of Diamond Grace seeps into the Earth and flows down rivers and streams into lakes and oceans. This Diamond Grace energy emitting from you eventually reaches the entire surface of the Earth Star. This beautiful energy that is water-filled and grace-filled nurtures the fertile soils and is taken up by the roots of these seeds seeking the light of our sun.

The cycle repeats itself, but now that you are in a state of grace you are assisting the Earth Star to perpetuate more units of consciousness filled with grace. Place your hand on your heart sealing in this energy of Diamond Grace and allow it to overflow within and radiates out. Trust in the Divine process of rebirth, and renewal, and that in each now moment, you radiate grace and are loved and appreciated for all that you are. State this affirmation out loud to integrate grace into the cycles of your daily life, "With love, grace, and compassion, I am Diamond Grace."

Grace Allows You to Stay at Peace and Emit a Prism of Calmness

Diamond Grace is like a shield. If you stay in a peaceful, graceful state in your heart, you can calm the world around you. When you are in a state of grace and there is caustic energy in the outside world, or you are around someone who is filled with angst and speaking with static energy coming out of their voice, mouth, and heart, use this natural impenetrable shield of your Diamond Grace to stay grounded. Stay centered, ground the light from above, and let this light illuminate the Diamond Grace grid that has overlaid your physical body.

When you are maintaining the state of grace these prisms of light reflect off of you. As altercations come within your personal space, these light rays refract off and naturally bring peace and calm to those before you, around you, and in your physical home or work environment. It's a ripple effect of these beautiful light rays filled with grace that can naturally radiate and assist others to absorb this peace and perhaps maintain a state of peace, at least within your presence.

You can also radiate grace to nature if you are outside and a storm is before you, the same light refracting from you is filled with grace. It is calming the elements of your outer world. It's calming the sky, the water, the fire element, and perhaps easing an angry storm, softening the rain. As you walk upon the path of a trail, your footsteps leave an imprint of grace, a light-filled imprint. The light is left in your footsteps and goes into the Earth and the soil. It helps to replenish the landscape with the light of grace bringing more units of luminescent light.

The animal kingdom, bird kingdom, and the sea creatures make their homes in the grace-filled landscape that you have created, and they too are receiving this luminescent light. They are now spreading this light wherever they fly, swim, or hop. Their offspring now carry this luminescent light of grace. This Divine Radiance will eventually cover the Earth Star. The momentum is created by you. We encourage you to go out in nature, go out in your city, your town, and just be: Be the radiant grace-filled being that you are. Your momentum is powerful.

Amplify and Ripple Out the Grace that Already Resides in Nature

Grace is grounding the light from above, from your light stream, from the higher octave, and into the center of your heart where a tiny flame resides. As you stream this light from above into your heart, this flame grows. This is a sacred flame. It is unseen. This is what builds the luminosity within.

In the higher octaves, love and light are the same. As you expand the love and light within, you become a shadowless being of light and love where higher frequencies and vibrations draw out the lower vibrations of the outer world. These higher vibrations and frequencies emanate a sound of the Divine. This is a state of bliss, joy, and ultimately grace.

You can stay in a state of grace with the world around you.

Nature is already filled with grace. You can be in grace by walking amongst a forest, or a park, or along the edge of a lake on a nature trail. This is walking in your connection to Source as

Source. This is heaven on Earth. This is the state you wanted to achieve. This is mastery over the mortal body. This is the introduction to the state of eternality, your eternal nature to be on the Earth Star in a heavenly state of grace.

Your Natural State is to Manifest Your Desires

As you connect more and more deeply with the cycles of the Earth and Mother Nature, you will come to know your own true eternal nature more deeply. You are the creator of your life experiences, and through your internal state of mind and heart, your emotional and mental state, you are emanating frequencies that desire a match that will be attracted to you. This is the natural state of your eternal being. If you wish to have a particular experience, you must state that intention. Your voice is the power of your creations. With these higher vibrations and frequencies, you manifest quickly for you do not have the lower vibrations of doubt or lack clouding these intentions. If you desire peaceful solutions or a joyful journey, just state these intentions out loud.

You naturally have this Source of Love and Light within that will infuse your thoughts and words. If you wish to have enlightened friends or partners, they will be attracted to your light. Intend this with your words. Choose your words wisely. There may be work to do in your consciousness or belief system. There's an up-leveling, a clarifying, in the belief system now. There is an infusion of light into lower vibrational thoughts that occur. Be mindful of the impact of your words or your thoughts. Gaze in the mirror and claim your beauty, your radiance.

It is like that analogy explaining that what you see is what you get. See the beauty. See that you are worthy of grace. Accept and express grace in all your now moments. Accept and express beauty in all your now moments. Accept and express joy in all your now moments. Claim the new job position you wish you have. Claim the relationships you wish to experience. Claim the abundance that is already yours.

Step out of survival consciousness and step up into the abundance that is before you. If you perhaps cannot see it in the physical yet, know it is there. Believe it is there. Trust that it is there. The power in your words, desire, and intentions will manifest in your personal experience. When you are ready to step into this power of grace, intention, and your voice, the universe responds in a form of synchronicity. A new career may fall into your lap. A conversation over coffee may bring you a new friendship.

You have a Divine team supporting you. Your angels and your guides are here arranging your future now moments to be bespoke for your desires and your intentions. They are here for you. You have the power. It is your Divine birthright. You are that special. You are that powerful. You are the Divine Child of God.

Uplevel Your Belief System and Your Words

You have been conditioned to say, "I am not worthy. I am not good enough. I will never have this or that. That person is too good for me." There is a settling consciousness too. "This is all I need. This will suit us for now." If this is your experience, therefore it is so. You can only have what you believe, say, or think. Let this resonate with you for a moment and understand you have been in control the whole time.

These words you are reading have been infused with nourishing energies to soften the transition, to change, uplevel, and infuse your beliefs with abundance and desire. Desire could be a new frequency in your system. It is okay to desire more for yourself. It is okay to desire more love, joy, beauty, money, laughter, or peace. You can start with simple intentions to help evolve your internal belief system.

Affirmations: Manifest Your Desires

You can choose daily affirmations to support these desires,

to affirm and anchor in these new, powerful, grace-filled ways of being. Affirm that you are a beautiful light-filled being. Affirm that you are worthy of all that you desire and require. Affirm that you are worthy of heaven on Earth.

"I desire more love to be in all my life experiences. I desire more money into my bank accounts. I desire a career that fulfills me. I desire friendships that uplift me. I desire a home environment that is beautiful. I desire a deeper connection to all that is around me."

Everyday Opportunities are Presented to Bring You Further into the State of Grace

We are infusing this with the frequency of wholeness and assisting you to bridge the gap and to take that leap. We will uplevel the facets of grace and all the elements of the Earth to infuse this container.

This is the Diamond Grace galaxy coming in to infuse these final words and codes. Your daily life mirrors your internal state of grace. Every day boulders can be put on your path providing opportunities to be in a state of grace. Every day invites a new opportunity to take a step forward on the path of being in a state of grace. If you trip and fall, just pick yourself up and continue with your desires, your intentions, and your affirmations. Until the entire Earth Star has been completely illuminated and all are living in a state of grace, there will be opportunities to show you where grace does not exist.

Continue to shine your radiance and your light of grace. Continue to let it resonate out. Achieving the state of grace is simply letting what is not grace fall away. Stay ever forward on this path for you are illuminating all that comes into your personal life experience. We are on this path with you. We champion you. You are appreciated more than you know beyond which your eyes can see.

Conclusion

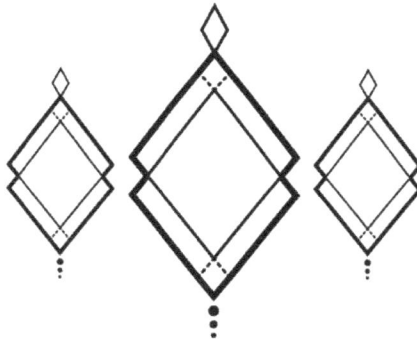

Being the Eight-Faceted Diamond
of Grace

Becoming a Diamond Under Pressure

Diamonds, which are considered very precious on the Earth Star and in the cosmic galaxy, start as carbon. They start as very dense material. It takes many, many, many years embedded deep in the Earth to be formed. As it sits in this space there is a lot of pressure placed upon it from the chaotic atmosphere of the Earth Star. As the tectonic plates shift and move there is a refine-ment of this element. It eventually turns into a crystalline diamond, a crystal clear, multifaceted stone. It is still held deep within the Earth. The only way to discover it is to dig on average at least one hundred miles into the surface of the Earth and uncover it.

This process is very deep and internal, much like what is happening within your physical body, your emotional body, and your mental body. These intense pressures of the outer world (and perhaps you can include your multiple incarnations) are adding to the refinement of your physical body, your carbon-based body. This carbon-based body can become more of a silicone-based body making it more crystalline in nature, more multifaceted where it can absorb and reflect light creating a luminosity, a luminous radiance in your auric field.

Your journey through this book has been an accelerated path of forming your inner diamond of radiance and grace and of bringing radiance and clarity to eight primary areas of your life, the eight facets of Diamond Grace. As you carry and bring forth Diamond Grace beyond the pages of this book, you will continue to unearth your radiance through the process of youthing—radiant beauty and physical radiance. Grace will take residence in your purpose, superpowers, and gifts, guiding you along the way. Your money and abundance will continue to grow and glow. Your life and relationships will be more joy-filled and radiant. Your connection with Source and nature will deepen. Through this journey together in the pages of Diamond Grace, you have resurrected the Diamond Grace grid within your system and your light quotient has dramatically increased. Grace and radiance in all areas of your life are the touchstones of your experience moving forward.

Your Birthright is Being in a State of Grace

This is your birthright. This is how you were born. This is the blueprint or the game plan for any incarnation on the Earth Star, but density over the years has clouded that over. As you personally change your inner landscape to become more crystalline, you also uncover these facets of your birthright, of the ways of living upon the Earth Star, the ways the humans were created originally.

This was the state of grace in which you would have these eight facets living a harmonious and joyful life. Reconnecting with these facets joins you with these ways of experiencing life upon planet Earth regardless of what is occurring around you. It's like a diamond sitting amongst the other elements unencumbered.

The Universe Amplifies the Greatest Expression of You

You experience the eight facets all in synchronicity and perhaps slowly like a small trickle that gains momentum. The facets all work together; as you have more abundance, you may have more time. As you have more time, you may be in nature more. As you are reconnecting to what makes you happy, you may become more beautiful and radiant. It continues to snowball. When you amplify your soul purpose there is an even deeper alchemical process that occurs within your sacred energetic centers.

As your soul connects to its original star, you become more divinely connected to that which you know, what is innate within your Divine blueprint, your Divine design. Living your life with Divine purpose causes deep joy within. Bringing your gifts and talents to humanity and to all the kingdoms on Earth at this time is the greatest gift that you can give. The universe gives back to you in kind, and this further amplifies the radiance and the grace, and the beauty that you contain.

Living your life *with* purpose *on* purpose helps create vitality, exuberance, and a zest for life. Getting outdoors and outside and communicating with other people and with Source, your guardians, and your guides creates a greater sense of community and wellness. Empower yourself. Be your authentic self. Be full out. We, the Diamond Grace galaxy see you, and it is our greatest desire to walk amongst you as you live the greatest expression of you as possible.

Call Upon the Diamond Grace Galaxy and We Will Assist You

It is our greatest joy to reconnect with you. We are here ever-present and listening, waiting for your voice. Call out in the silence or with the spoken word and we will be with you. We shall come and assist you with all your requests, dreams, and desires to bring luminosity to your physical body and to assist your auric field to radiate with Divine light. You are not alone. There is a whole galaxy waiting for your intention, your call, and your desire to reconnect to your original state of grace.

It is as simple as setting an intention and then allowing the light to come to you. Be open and receptive. Be patient with yourself. Be kind to yourself. Radiance illuminating your physical body is indeed an alchemical process and does not happen overnight, but surely it is occurring on a microcosmic level. Breathing, stretching, and spending time in moments of silence allow the alchemy of radiance to process in your biological system.

If it is your intention to reconnect even more deeply to the state of grace and increase the luminosity within your biological system, we can offer a few words to assist with this. You can also use your own words. We encourage you to use words that are unique and bespoke for your system because every diamond is unique. We wish to honor that. All diamonds are not crystal clear. There are diamonds with many aspects of color variations. They are all beautiful.

To connect with us is quite simple. It is just basing your intention on your inner desire to be more luminous and to seek this radiant light from the Diamond Grace galaxy. There we instantly hear your call and send a stream of light directly to your heart center in this now moment of your calling. We wish for you to amplify it with more intention and affirmations. This helps your neurological system to create the momentum necessary.

Affirmations: Connect with Diamond Grace

"I wish to connect with the Diamond Grace galaxy, with Diamond Grace, with the angels and masters from this great cosmic place in our universe. I wish to connect to the light that you are offering and to bring it into my heart center. I allow this light to expand and grow within my physical, emotional, and mental bodies. I ask you to watch over me and to expand this light and increase its radiance every moment. Expand the luminosity from within and out into my auric field. I wish for my multi-body system to radiate out into this outer world where I reside.

"I wish to become a multifaceted diamond with Diamond Grace. I wish to experience the eight facets in my daily life unencumbered by the outer world. I trust and I know that this light is nourishing my physical body and bringing me into a state of grace. My original Divine blueprint is contained within the state of grace. My DNA is fully illuminated. Daily I will reflect upon the radiance within my heart and the nourishment that you, Diamond Grace, are providing me. Daily I will affirm that I am a radiant being expressing my light upon this Earth Star. I am so grateful, and I am blessed to be resourced by your radiance every day. I thank you."

This is Diamond Grace. We will truly be with you every moment. Your radiance will grow, illuminate, and increase every moment if this is your desire. We encourage you to be all that you are. Our love for you is Divine. It is our greatest honor to reconnect with you and to bring your state of being into wholeness, into oneness, and to assist you to express all that you are. Our love is eternal and so are you.

Honor Your Process and Perfect Path

The gestation period of the embodiment of Diamond Grace is not measurable within the human construct of time. We can say that the foot on the gas, the acceleration, depends on the individual effort or pressure of the foot on the pedal. It would be counterproductive to happen in an instant as it would be too much for the human flesh, the biological structure. It is more like a slow trickle. You do not want to overload the lightbulb and have it burst.

Each human is unique in their enlightenment process as in how much light they have internalized or how much density they have cleared in their multi-body system. It is unique for each, but do not think that it isn't possible. The evolution of your radiant light body begins when you initiate the process. Enjoy the process. Do not compare yourself with others. Maybe they initiated the process years before you. That does not make it different or any less. There should be no comparison.

Perhaps your years of embodiment are not the same. Perhaps it was part of your purpose to experience 3D situations allowing you to experience a deeper sense of compassion. The path that you are on is perfect and it is your path. Honor that path and your life experience. It is all on purpose, for purpose. The time in which full radiance or a state of grace exists for you in your personal experience is your unique journey. We would like to say that once you begin the journey you have already begun in this book, you are already in a state of grace.

You've Resurrected and Ignited Your Diamond Grace Grid

The frequencies and codes are all here and have been activated. The words are encoded deeply with vibrations and frequencies from the Diamond Grace galaxy and perhaps you have felt them. It is a free-will world and intention is the only way to clearly allow these to come into your experience. You allow the initiation process to occur.

"I have accepted the frequencies, codes, and vibrations emanating from the pages of this book. I accept the nourishing life from Diamond Grace and the Diamond Grace galaxy. I am walking upon the Earth Star in a state of grace in all now moments. So be it, and so it is."

We, the Ascended Masters, angels, gods, and goddesses that are a part of this book are honored and grateful to engage with you in this way. We also offer our eternal love and abundant resources to you in all your now moments. You may also call on us at any time and we will assist you on your path through grace. We are honored to greet you and to make ourselves known if you have not been familiar with who we are. We are real as you are. We are offering our gifts and our Divine light to nurture and support you always. We thank you. You are loved, and all is love.

About the Author

Terri is an author, Certified Quantum Light Practitioner, and member of the Ascended Master lineage of Thoth via Danielle Rama Hoffman.

In 2014, through her direct connection with Source, Diamond Grace–a new Earth modality–came here to begin their mission to reconnect humans to grace. It was revealed to Terri while in communication that the State of Grace was a period that humans were in and collectively decided to disconnect from millions of years ago.

Diamond Grace illuminates pathways for sacred journeys within and empower you to evolve how you view yourself. Through grace and compassion, they assist you in finding solace and awakening your internal radiance using Quantum Light.

Dedicated and unwavering, Terri has traveled to many sacred

sites known and unknown to create portals and grids to facilitate the newly resourced streams of consciousness that are here to increase cosmic love and light.

She assists clients around the globe to unearth the restorative superpowers of Diamond Grace to reclaim physical radiance, beauty, and abundance and lead them toward their best life. She scribes books and sacred geometry that she hopes will reach everyone seeking a beautiful and abundant life.

You can work with Terri and Diamond Grace through 1:1 mentoring, and group programs dedicated to support your Return to Radiance, including the Eight Facets of Diamond Grace, to experience an extraordinary, meaningful life, and the personalized Resurrection of Immortality program. To find out more go to LightInfusions.com.

For more great books visit Scribes of Light online at
Books.GracePointPublishing.com

SCRIBES OF LIGHT
PRESS

If you enjoyed reading Return to Radiance and purchased it through an online retailer, please return to the site and write a review to help others find this book.

www.ingramcontent.com/pod-product-compliance
Lightning Source LLC
Chambersburg PA
CBHW031141090426
42738CB00008B/1177